TEACHER

Touch Their Futures

VICTOR SGAMBATO

CONTENTS

- A look back at my surprisingly delighted and heartwarming entry into the world of teaching.
- Additionally, a description of the book's contents.

Section I: <u>You</u> Retain the Potential to Inspire, Motivate, & Support Your Students.

- Designed to remind the readers of the many **rewards** attained from their chosen profession. Through sharing some of my classroom experiences, I wish to underscore a teacher's formidable role, reminding you of your potential influence upon the many students encountered in your career.

- I describe extraordinary days within my career that I recall with considerable emotion. Despite some of their conflicting natures, they may, nevertheless, inspire you to reflect upon <u>your own</u> meaningful encounters and consider the endless possibilities of sensitive episodes yet to be experienced within your career.

- The next chapter is based upon the importance generated by **fellowship** and **support** as it may exist among colleagues and how it affects one's students. When teachers work together, engaging professional development, it is an excellent beginning. When they become better personally acquainted in a relaxed, non-structured environment away from the classroom, significant bonding often sets in. With the merging of both encounters, I believe that educators tend to more easily develop as a unified **team** and are better able to sincerely affect the academic, as well as personal lives of their students. Relationships are enhanced, friendships develop, and everyone benefits, especially the kids.

Section II: Professional Advice in Dealing With Your Students.

- Sixteen experiential lessons helping teachers in dealing with their students. Experience is usually acquired through years of on the job encounters. This chapter, however, will give the new teacher a bit of a "head start" while offering the experienced teacher an opportunity to review one's teaching style.

Section III: Tools that Succeed: Unconventional Approaches and Strategies

- Unconventional strategies are suggested for you to consider using in your classroom. Proposed are **unique, unorthodox** methods and procedures which creatively acquire the students' undivided attention and more easily motivate their thought processes. The students can thus be drawn into the lesson by instinct and interest. What could be better! Examples are described.

- Occasionally, a student may approach the teacher seeking, advice, attention, understanding, even safety…and most importantly, someone willing to **listen**. This chapter proposes the use of a specific list of listening skills which works very effectively on those occasions (along with reasons why your response is so important).

- Recommendations are offered as to how an educator may go about adjusting his/her listening techniques in an effort to remove barriers that frequently stand in the way of solid communication. Also clarified are reasons why giving comfort and support to a student in need is so important.

- Chapter 8 offers lessons and activities designed to develop a **Cooperative Environment** within the classroom. In this setting, (advocating teamwork) the skills of community effort and mutual learning are established and enhanced. These unique approaches are intended to open students' minds to the need for **sensitivity** and **cooperation** in life when dealing with peers as well as the danger and uselessness of **intimidation** and **bullying**. Included are some of the rewarding and exceptionally successful approaches and activities I experienced during my career.

- Continuing in a similar direction as described in chapter 8, the Seat of Distinction is intended to help students develop mutual respect for each other while also avoiding self-criticism. The lesson focuses upon sincere **compliments** exchanged with peers.

- Approaches are intended to open students' minds to the need for **sensitivity, trust, and comfort** when dealing with peers as well as focusing once more upon the worthlessness of **intimidation, bullying, and self-depreciation.** Fairness and equality may be pursued in class discussions and stressed frequently by the teacher. Additionally, students take part in classroom conversations based upon the potential damage and repercussions of **self-criticism.** Incorporated are several activities and approaches proven to be effective and very satisfying in my career.

-Sensitivity to feelings of peers + reduction of self-deprecation = less bullying, more environmental comfort, and greater academic success-

- **Testimony is offered by former students that had taken part in the <u>Seat of Distinction</u> earlier in their lives.**

<u>Is There More That Can We Do?</u>

- Included within is my declaration that when given opportunities to be of service to others, our young people can be resourceful, successful, and happy to be involved in affecting the school, their classmates, and the community in positive ways. Through experiencing opportunities that meet with success, they come to realize just how valuable each can be.

- They are also offered the opportunity to work on leadership skills which may be used within the school setting as well as in life.

- This approach could be easily utilized by educators

employed in school systems which evaluate their teachers, in part, by requiring involvement in community responsibilities.

- Targeting a vulnerable age group, this concept introduces the kids to a setting where they may begin interacting and building trust in a sheltered environment. The sessions are organized in an effort to give the youths a forum within which to express, explore, and better understand ensuing emotions, while also recognizing that they are not alone in experiencing misgivings and reservations. Students attending such sessions can learn more about the world of adolescence, acquire skills to successfully deal with personal concerns, and experience pride and satisfaction when being of help to classmates.

Testimony is offered by former members who are now adults.

- Our students, too frequently, regard the unfamiliar with suspicion and aversion. A logical strategy to employ, therefore, would be to acquaint our kids with those cultures that may appear unfamiliar to them. Our young people should be allowed to see evidence that ethnic groups from many parts of the world have made significant contributions to the American experience. And because of these multicultural achievements, we share a kinship with one another.
- The ultimate goals of this chapter are: The reduction of possibly prejudiced thoughts and discriminating behaviors among class members and an understanding and acceptance of cultural diversity. The curriculum and activities promote tolerance, equality, fairness, mutual respect for all people, and even an appropriate first-hand reaction to discrimination.

Testimony is included from former class members who are now, as adults, members of the teaching profession.

The Last Chapter:
- Offers the reader some indication as to what it may be like to exit the profession; the emotional journey, the loss, as well as the gratification of knowing that the voyage through the world of child-centered teaching was correct, satisfying, and totally enjoyed.

FORWARD

KEYS TO SUCCESSFUL AND REWARDING TEACHING

Reading this book will change how you look at the art of teaching. I say art because every teacher brings a style and approach to the classroom that is unique.

The new teacher will read these pages looking for ideas that have proven successful in the classroom. Seasoned teachers will use the ideas expressed within this book to validate their techniques or expand and improve their approach.

As you read, you will discover that Mr. Sgambato is dedicated to a student centered classroom approach. He is a firm believer that you must create an environment that allows the student to perform with a high level of self-confidence. His methods and lessons, as he has presented them in this book, have proven highly effective.

I believe that Mr. Sgambato's message is, *if you are well prepared, student centered, and comfortable in your own skin, you will experience the Joys of Teaching.*

Walt Wheeler, retired school principal, (and former adjunct professor with the University of Phoenix)

ACKNOWLEDGMENT

This book was made possible by the support, encouragement, and guidance of the following colleagues:

Mike Gifford
Tom Murray
Walt Wheeler
Carol Edwards
Myrna Herb
Kurt Fetter
Gretta Smith
Carol Green
Maryanne Brookman
Jeanne DeValve

Mike and Tom, the two gentlemen at the top of the list, were in a position to provide me with a remarkably generous amount of patience, honesty, and amazing assistance. The information contained within the book would not measure up nearly as well as it does without them. Tom and Mike, thank you so much for your gracious time and support.

Walt Wheeler, formerly our school principal, adjunct professor with the University of Phoenix, author of my book's Foreword, and good friend. Thank you for your ongoing support, patience, and useful advice throughout my teaching career and during the construction of this book.

And lastly, a heartfelt thank you to all the wonderful young people that entered my life for thirty-five years. I cannot imagine having done anything else for a living. As Harvey Mackay (motivational speaker and author) stated, "If you love your job, you never work a day in your life."

INTRODUCTION

It's early morning. You're standing near the open door of your classroom awaiting the arrival of your students. As they make their way down the corridor, the noise level slowly begins to rise. They enter, and a short time later, the sound of a bell pierces the air and their conversations. Chattering all but comes to an end. Bill and Eddie, sitting in the back of the room, continue whispering for a few seconds. You remain standing, waiting, eyes floating across the group of alert faces. Bill nods at Eddie, and Eddie smiles...both turn their attention toward you, joining the rest of the class as they await your first words.

They're ready. You're ready. You're prepared, happy, energized, and thankful,.... What would you do without them? Here we go! Hit them loudly, unconventionally, with words of unique interest.... Make them smile, make them listen, **captivate** their attention and begin your interaction.

Do you like kids? (Do bears live in the woods?)

As a professional teacher, you, no doubt, enjoy immersing your students in daily lessons. Would you like to encourage even greater academic passion, interact with them more enthusiastically, and be extraordinarily influential in touching their futures? Then, this book would be advantageous.

There are approximately three million public school teachers in classrooms today with an additional 310,000 entering the profession yearly. Most would agree, I believe, that they can certainly use some valuable classroom suggestions. In my book, I offer practical advice and stimulating, educational approaches rarely available in text form. Additionally, I include an assortment of touching memoirs designed to encourage readers in recalling their own poignant classroom encounters.

My intended audience would be... the <u>new</u> teacher, the mid-career teacher, as well as the teacher having completed decades in the profession. Realistically, this book's audience includes **<u>any</u> professional educator engaged** in this grand vocation with a desire to educate and motivate one's students while simultaneously appreciating this incredible adventure of teaching our young. For those following <u>The Common Core Standards</u>, techniques within these pages are applicable in that they help develop an appropriate environment conducive to entering this challenging setting.

Today's students are graduating into a world of unprecedented change filled with challenges necessitating unique and inspiring scholastic techniques on the part of their teachers. Many of our educational styles and approaches demand appropriate modifications, developed in a manner so as to vigorously motivate our pupils. Standard approaches frequently waste time and bar progress, leaving many of our students short of reaching potential academic success, and too often, unaware of education's benefits.

My primary desire in writing this book is to offer personal advice with suggestions utilizing appropriate, educational strategies. After thirty-five years in the profession, I am convinced that it is of most importance to build strong relationships of **respect** and **trust** with your pupils, while utilizing stimulating methods of academic and personal **interaction.**

In a society that is moving so rapidly, I believe that today's students are in need of stronger, more effective motivation. Approaches offered in my book contain inspiring, unorthodox educational techniques that will encourage your kids to sincerely appreciate the advantages of your academic efforts.

Another of my goals is to remind you of the many delights derived from your chosen career. Through sharing of my classroom encounters, I wish to remind you of your own compelling influence upon the many students you've inspired in your career. I urge you to reflect upon your many meaningful encounters while considering the endless possibility of significant, sensitive episodes yet to be experienced within your time in the classroom.

CHAPTER 1: REFLECTIONS

"Is it true you're retiring at the end of this year?" Jan's chin rose a bit as she spoke; her eyes narrowed, and a slight wrinkle appeared on her brow. By December of 1999, word of my impending retirement had apparently reached the ears of my sixth-grade students. Jan had always been a free-spirited and totally blunt young lady. I was not surprised at all that it was she who first had the courage to ask about my decision to leave the profession.

After a short pause, I responded, "Those are my plans, Jan."

Her body tipped back a bit, face somewhat ashen and eyes glassy. Then, a pause, followed by, "But what about all the other kids?" Her words hit me hard. Not only was I unprepared for the flattering nature of that emotional question; it also caused me to reflect suddenly and seriously upon the finality of my decision. The room was silent as I moved slowly toward her desk and placed my hand on her shoulder. Looking into her eyes, all I could manage was a bit of a half-smile, as I offered, "My thoughts exactly." However, my personal interpretation was, "What will I be missing?"

At a class event a few nights later, I was approached by Mrs. Hudsin. She remarked that she was "bummed" because of my upcoming retirement. She had a son in fourth grade and was looking forward to the day when I'd be his sixth-grade teacher. A few minutes following that, Mrs. Snyder made very similar comments. I knew that my absence would make little difference in the final "student product." It was, however, totally rewarding and passionately moving to see that there were individuals who believed that, with my leaving, something would be missing in terms of student experiences. I felt overwhelmed. Again, it occurred to me just how emotionally difficult the move was going to be. On my way home that evening, my thoughts drifted to a time thirty-five years earlier.

It was midsummer, 1961. I was nineteen years old. After graduating from high school that June, I'd assumed that my classroom time had come to an end. I stood in the middle of the road watching a football as it drifted slowly toward the ground ten feet to my right. I slid over and caught it. A second later, however, I was tagged by one of my friends from the opposing team. We made our way to the center of the road to prepare for a third down. We'd been playing touch football in the middle of Third Street in Gloversville, New York, for years. Enjoying the game as we always did, it easily absorbed our full attention. Therefore, we were rather jolted when my mother suddenly appeared on the front porch of our home, adjacent to the game. She was holding the door open with one hand and waving a letter in the other while shouting, "You have an appointment at Castleton State College next Friday." I'd never heard of Castleton State College and had no idea what she was referring to.

Later that day, I found that she'd signed my name to an interview request form that she'd acquired weeks earlier. I had an appointment with a Professor Gilbert. I saw, however, no reason to travel to Vermont. Working at a local mill for nearly $2.10 an hour, I was quite content with my life. Though I invested twelve hours a day, six days a week, re-directing my life seemed unnecessary. As far as I was concerned, my future was blossoming and full of promise. Nevertheless, a week later, we were on our way to the Vermont border.

I'd agreed to take part in the interview solely to satisfy my mother. After all, when Professor Gilbert took a look at my 73.4 high school average, he would have little desire to waste his time on me.

The interview was surprisingly pleasant. Mr. Gilbert asked me questions based upon the world of children and education; I answered them as honestly as I could. Unexpectedly, the longer we spoke, the more interested I became in his questions...and the more absorbed I became in the conversation. Following the interview, we returned to Gloversville. I did not expect to ever return to Vermont. Two weeks later, however, I received word that I had been accepted at Castleton State Teachers' College. Classes were to begin at the end of August. I quit my job.

COLLEGE

During my first two years at Castleton State College, I had many entertaining encounters. The occasions, needless to say, were social events rather than classroom experiences. One could easily tell by simply viewing my poor grade index. Then, in my junior year, I began taking education courses,…and for the first time, experienced student teaching. The good times then transformed into *wonderful* times. A new and different world opened to me. I'd anticipated that spending time as the center of attention in an open classroom of kids might be interesting. However, after engaging the group of fourth- and fifth graders during my first student teaching experience, I could think of nothing else. It was amazing! I focused, I prepared lessons, I learned. The education courses I'd taken began to truly make sense. My grades during the two remaining years of college never fell below a 3.0, and I comfortably felt that I was headed in the right direction. I'd never experienced such a wonderful feeling. During the second semester of student teaching in my senior year, the following thought occurred: "Someday, they were actually going to pay me *money* to do this thing I loved, called "Teaching." I found it incredible.

After completing all student teaching requirements and several remaining education courses, I ultimately found myself riding home with diploma in hand, pondering to which area schools I should apply.

A few weeks later, as I pulled out of the Fort Plain Central School parking lot, the reality of the last two hours began to sink in. My meeting with the elementary principal and district superintendent had concluded with an offer to teach the sixth grade. I'd signed the contract with no hesitation whatsoever— (after all, $5,000 a year sounded amazing!). On the drive home, I smiled, I laughed, I sang. In two short months, I would be standing in front of twenty-seven eager ten and eleven year- olds with futures that I could potentially and positively affect.

What had I ever done to deserve the wonderful experience awaiting me?

———————————— **(Thanks, Mom)** ————————————

Are you a teacher? Might that be a *new* teacher...a mid-career teacher...a teacher near retirement? What motivated you to enter the profession? More than likely, it was the salary, right? OK, OK, I'll be serious. Honestly, what is it that the classroom offers you? If you are doing, in life, what you were meant to do... if you indeed enjoy teaching, then you, more than likely, have your own relevant response to this question readily available.

While engaged in this grand profession, you have the advantage of being of supreme service in a most satisfying way...touching the future of countless young people as they live their lives. You retain the potential to educate, to influence, to motivate, to persuade. You offer a lesson of interest, a supportive comment, a gesture, a look, a touch, ...none of which you may remember with the passing of only a few minutes;... the young recipients of your encouragement, however, may be able to easily recall the experience and resulting emotions years from that day. What you say, how you say it, how you dress, how you smile, IF you smile.... We can never be totally certain how our interaction with these young people will ultimately affect their education, inspiration, mood, ability to persevere, capacity to find comfort in who they truly are—but there is *always* that powerful potential to do so.

As my former colleague, Gary Kuch, would say, "You never have no effect on others." ...and who might be more impressionable than a group of eager students sitting in your classroom....? _____

WHAT IS THIS BOOK ABOUT?

The interior contains thirteen chapters within <u>four</u> sections:

1. *You* Retain the Potential to Inspire, Motivate, and Support Your Students.
2. Professional Advice for Dealing with Your Students.
3. Tools That Succeed: Unconventional Approaches and Strategies
4. What More Can We Do?

A CLOSER LOOK:

1. You **Retain the Potential to Inspire, Motivate, and Support**
I've included an assortment of reflective, personal encounters experienced in my successful thirty-five-year career in education which I trust will emotionally move the reader to familiar depths of professional gratification and pride in being a teacher. The descriptions are designed to encourage a recollection of your own poignant episodes in the classroom, thus reminding all teachers of the splendid delight they enjoy in being educators. The professional joys you attain help underscore your role in possessing the potential to positively affect the many students that enter your arena of instruction. Take the opportunity to reflect upon your own memorable classroom achievements.

2. Professional Advice in Dealing with Your Students
This section contains personal advice to consider when spending so much of your life in the classroom. I offer suggestions supporting effective ways to build strong connections of respect and trust with your students. Many are unconventional,…as standard, familiar behavior patterns, employed by too many teachers, often waste time and bar progress. These proposals will be immensely useful in getting your students on board if you are following the **Common Core Standards**.

3. Tools That Succeed: Unconventional Approaches and Strategies

A collection of unique lessons, approaches, and professional strategies containing what I believe are inspiring, unorthodox, and very effective educational styles. These unconventional methods serve to acquire the students' undivided attention, influence their desire to learn as well as their self-esteem, and creatively motivate their thought processes in a variety of successful, academic ventures. They work!

4. What More Can We Do?

Three chapters offering unconventional lessons and projects suggesting ways for your students to:

- Affect the school, their peers, and the community in positive ways, improving the climate and making things better.

- Help other class members experience opportunities to meet with success.

- Work on leadership skills useful in school and in life.

- Express their genuine feelings, discuss emotional issues while building confidence and self-esteem.

- Experience pride and self-respect, as well as perceive their own potential value.

- Determine ways to avoid insecurity, low self-esteem, anger, and violence.

- Enhance multicultural acceptance, counter the existence of bigotry, and work together in understanding, accepting, and celebrating different cultural traditions.

———

- In chapters 6 through 9, in section 3, I've included a number of actual classroom lessons that were quite valuable to me. In the written text, I incorporate what I consider to be useful, detailed components applied to the development of each lesson. Though I feel that the chapter details are necessary in an initial comprehension of the curricula, if, at a later time, the reader would like to simply engage an organized, user-friendly "lesson plan" version of each activity, it can be found in the appendix.

I designed my comments to inspire; to encourage you to view your professional life, teaching responsibilities, and especially your students in a unique, exciting, and thankful manner. Additionally, I've endeavored to give you cause to ponder; to speculate as to the capabilities and the significant potential of the average adolescent. I'm eager to discuss their behavior and views of life at these sometimes-difficult ages, as well as some of the astonishing achievements attained when they are given the opportunities.

"I HAVE SO LITTLE TIME!"

It's possible that some readers may feel that there isn't sufficient time to present the "preparatory lessons" I've included within chapters 8 and 9 (Cooperative Environment and Seat of Distinction). I understand the concern. However, please consider the following: The lessons have a common purpose. Their intention is to blend the students into an effective team possessing common goals while learning within a collaborative setting. The result is a group of youngsters with a shared understanding of their roles, responsibilities, and the determination to work together successfully. As for sufficient time to teach the lessons, wouldn't it be more credible to think of these molding activities as a time-saving investment for the future?

If you're successful in grooming the students…coaching and preparing them for their nine and one-half months in your classroom—won't that **save** precious time later? If you're able to do away with many of the typical classroom obstructions,..the misbehaviors, disagreements, withdrawals, displays of anger, lack of effort,…won't the educational experiences blend together more easily, move along more successfully? A greater possibility will exist that the students will be on the same page as their teacher. You're not wasting time in offering these activities. You're being conscientious and better organized.

I believe that many of the methods used in my classroom during a thirty-five year career would be worthy of consideration on the part of contemporary teachers. They worked for me as well as many of my colleagues. Take a look; see what you think.

Though it does not necessarily follow that you have the need or the freedom to engage every one of them, the strong possibility does remain that you will find a number of the encounters valuable and wish to productively utilize them. Read about the concepts and philosophies as I employed them. This is how *I* did it. How much of it useful to you?

In chapters 10, 11, and 12, I describe several exclusive projects that involved numerous groups of my students over the years. I honestly believe that they easily have the potential to provide valuable learning experiences and rewarding results for many of today's young people. I trust that these unique encounters offer an abundance of evidence as to what these youngsters can successfully comprehend as well as achieve.

SECTION ONE:

YOU RETAIN THE POTENTIAL TO INSPIRE, MOTIVATE, & SUPPORT

CHAPTER 2: JOYS OF TEACHING

JOY #1: CONTACT WITH FORMER STUDENTS

"Mr. Johnson, remember me, Joanne Freeman? You were my seventh-grade math teacher!"

From time to time, educators have the pleasure of making contact with former students. This could be through classroom visits or when unexpectedly meeting individuals who were members of a particular class two, six, ten or more years ago. If you've been in the profession for several years or longer, this has more than likely already occurred. When I'm fortunate enough to experience these occasions, it pleases me that I'm remembered…but what gives me even more satisfaction is when these folks recall something I did or said that they found themselves fondly remembering. If they share such an incident with me, I'm almost always caught off guard. I'll stumble for words, ultimately saying, "Thank you." I then attempt to let the individual know just how meaningful the experience is. No matter how difficult a day I may be having…regardless how stressed I may be feeling, these encounters quickly remind me of the grand rewards reaped from this delightful profession.

I was sitting at a table in a local auto garage waiting for my car to be serviced when a young man in his late twenties entered the room. His face was familiar, but I felt it was one that I hadn't seen in quite some time.

I concluded right away that, once again, I'd encountered a former student who had, naturally, put on a few years. He spotted me immediately, walked over and extended his hand, addressed me as, "Mr. Sgambato," and asked how I'd been. I quickly admitted that, though his face was very familiar, I'd most likely last seen it on a much smaller body. I honestly explained that I simply couldn't recall his name.

"Steve Jones," he quickly replied. I quietly stared and, as is the case with nearly all similar events, started to receive eighteen-year-old images in my mind featuring Steve Jones as an eleven-year-old...—short hair, slightly taller than most of his classmates, attentive. In my mental image, he watched me as I moved about the classroom...leaning forward a bit with both elbows on his desk. His head tilted slightly to one side, his facial expression offering evidence of total attention.

Steve sat with me and stated, "I was just thinking of you while driving yesterday..., and here you are today. Actually, I think of you often."

"Of my teaching or of my jokes?" I responded with a smile.

"Both," replied Steve, smiling back to me. He passed me a copy of *Country Folks*, a local community publication, and explained that he wrote for the paper. I opened to page two, and there it was, a story written by Steve. I read a bit of it, and noticed that the lead (opening sentence) was a "zinger," a "grabber." It immediately reached out to a reader and grabbed the individual's attention. I complimented him on his style.

As we chatted a bit, the shop's owner entered the room and explained that my car was ready to go. I bade good-bye to my former student and moved toward the counter at the opposite end of the room. Steve, then, called out my name and, as I turned toward him, said, "I remember how you got me interested in words... and in writing; thank you."

I replied, "Thank *you*, Steve; that means a lot to me. Take care..."

I never forget these gratifying experiences. To think that my leading a class down this interesting but somewhat challenging road to self-expression would result in this wonderful manner is so immensely satisfying. A number of readers will identify with this event, having more than likely enjoyed similar experiences. Then there are those rare occasions such as the one that follows:

About two years ago, I received a message in my voice mail from a young man I'd had in class a number of years ago. It began, "Hello, Mr. Sgambato. You probably don't remember me. You were my teacher in the sixth grade. You were my dad's teacher as well. My name is Keith Ferilli. I wanted to call and thank you because of what you gave me while in your class. It allowed me to go out and chase my dream job. Now, I have it. I'm currently an MP in the United States Army military police. And I wouldn't change it for all the money in the world. I thank you, sir. Bye." I absolutely do remember Keith. However, I cannot recall anything I might have done that contributed to his attaining his, "dream job."

Did I say something, do something, teach something that Keith found stirring,...inspiring,? I have no idea what it could have been. If one former student was motivated by something I unknowingly included in a lesson, could there be others as well? What about the students whom *you* inspired? How many have you run into? If not given the opportunity to cross paths with them, you'll not necessarily see evidence of your inspirations...but these people more than likely do exist.... Think about them....after all, they think about you....

When your lesson concludes, and the students gather their belongings to begin filing out of the room, could one or more still be thinking about your words, your suggestions, your motivation? Will those thoughts return to their minds later while on their way home or lying in bed that night? Could your influence actually cause some to later make future decisions based on their classroom experience? We may never know for certain, but there is always that potential. It is essential that we conduct our professional and personal lives while considering that likelihood.

JOY OF TEACHING #2: THE "TEACHER RUSH"

When was the last time you experienced the, "Teacher Rush?"... that moment when that *something special* happens in your lesson? You may lead students in a stimulating class conversation ending with an unexpected conclusion, or reveal a surprising detail about a particular subject...heads turn, eyes lift and sparkle, the room goes silent, students stare...all eyes are upon you. And you know...they're doing some heavy thinking...and most significantly, it was *you* who made them think! What a feeling! It's as though some kind of **magic** has occurred.

The **magic** is part of teaching. It lives in your classroom. I believe there's a way to access the phenomenon, re-experiencing and appreciating the sensation again: After a long day of teaching, stop at the door for a moment before exiting. (It works best when the building is quiet.) There is an essence of classroom magic that you can encounter again. Begin by looking around the room...slowly...taking in the walls, bulletin boards, desks, chairs.... Then focus upon the hands that were in the air, the stares, the questions, the comments, the enthusiasm, the laughter, the expressions on the faces of young people who had, at earlier moments of the day, perhaps, discovered something about math, science, English, home and career skills, social studies, technology, physical education, health, Spanish...that they found interesting, challenging, different. And you held their eyes, their attention, their interest, their education, perhaps even a small part of their future...in your hands...for a brief time. The room may be empty, but you can still perceive the phenomenon. The magic is there...just take the time, before leaving, to recall, to reminisce, to ***feel***.

We are given the opportunity to live on this planet for many reasons... foremost in importance, being of service to others. That's why many of us find ourselves in education. It's a wonderful way to satisfy that opportunity. "If you love your job, you never *work* a day in your life" (a phrase popularized by business writer Harvey Mackay), certainly applicable.

The late Arthur Ashe said, "From what we get, we can make a living; what we give, however, makes a life." You've entered one of the noblest professions...and you've succeeded; you're a teacher. You've touched many lives; your influence has spread. You deserve to be proud.

JOY OF TEACHING #3: INSPIRE YOUR STUDENTS

How? What's the best way? My opinion....

Involve them in the lesson...preferably by using a prepared, unconventional approach. If a teacher can acquire students' total attention and gain their sincere interest, it's likely that all will be moving side by side in the same academic direction. And... everyone will share the enjoyment.

Now, when I say "involve" your students, it entails more than simply listening to the teacher. It requires them to become totally **immersed, committed, absorbed,** and **determined** in the lesson. Certainly, Cooperative Learning is an effective way to begin, or you could use any other well-devised approach to attract and immediately engage the kids. Be creative in **hooking** them into the lesson. Then with a plan of _immersed_ involvement in mind, I frequently designed lessons to encourage large amounts of peer interaction among the kids, ...breaking them into teams of two while encouraging discussions centered upon the task at hand. After the teams discussed the subject and found potential directions to pursue in resolving the task, I combined each team with another unit of two and directed them to continue the dialogue as they developed additional information and individual opinions. Following this segment, we would engage in a "Community Meeting" involving the entire class. Within this setting, dialogue would transpire and the group would consider numerous solutions and opinions in pursuing the theme. Because of their personal involvement, they become more strongly focused on the lesson. With this approach, not only do students make academic progress, but they also develop more positive, cooperative social skills and build self-confidence. It works much better than a didactic lecture stemming solely from the teacher.

When young people talk together, they learn together, and consequently, progress together. Watch as the room fills with comments dealing with the task at hand. Enjoy the expressions, gestures, and involvement....

Tell me and I forget...

Show me, and I remember...

Involve me, and I learn! [1]

I believe this, and research supports it.

How can you foster that complete **involvement in the lesson?** Here are three methods I've successfully used.

KIDS WORKING TOGETHER, INVOLVED ---

THE WRITING PROCESS

This is one of my favorite approaches. In my writing classes, while emphasizing creativity and a free-writing spirit, I taught my pupils to respond immediately to *any* topic-related ideas by jotting them down as they occurred to them. Following that, they were to place the thoughts in a sensible *order*, then compose a rough draft based solely upon what they wanted to say as the information entered their heads. They were to pay little attention to the mechanics...grammar, spelling, and punctuation. I based much of each piece's evaluation upon particular writing skills (topic sentence, supporting sentences, vivid, descriptive words, the conveying of feelings... sadness, sympathy, etc.). After the author revised the draft for content only, two peer editors individually read the piece, also suggesting appropriate revisions for content. They discussed their opinions with the author. Following a second draft, within which the author revised the content to his or her satisfaction, students edited their own piece for mechanical errors, and the "writing skills" assigned. Finally, two different peers also edited the piece for mechanical errors and writing skills. The author then completed the final draft, making any adjustments he or she felt necessary.

The room was always filled with comments, discussions, and enjoyable, supporting conversations. Students worked together and learned together.

Rather than being assigned as homework, the majority of the composing took place within the controlled environment of the classroom. That helped contribute to their best effort. The final draft was a result of serious collaboration and combined effort by the author along with four helpful editors. The class collectively progressed. I graded the final drafts with each composer sitting next to me as I worked my way through the piece.

The learning was shared; the teaching was shared. When possible, the compositions were read to the class.

PUBLIC SPEAKING

Class members wrote down comments based upon each speaker's presentation during the delivery. Afterward, they gave the speaker both compliments and suggestions for improvement in an appropriate manner. The results were discussed, and speakers took notes on the suggestions. As they continued through their future speaking assignments, the improvements were obvious. Members of the class worked together, each taking on additional challenges. Consequently, working together, they were rigorously involved in the daily routine. They learned and shared what was absorbed from class members.

READING

In my reading classes, we read silently and orally. During the oral reading, students were urged to study and interpret the author's meaning and intention, then orally deliver the words for their classmates in whatever appropriate way they felt met the author's intent.

There were also occasions when my classes would discuss the author's use of imagery, foreshadowing, character development, flashback techniques, and so on in small group settings. After opinions were formed and discussed, they were then shared and debated by the entire class. I did my best to involve everyone. They worked together. They learned together. Through performing in this manner with everyone actively involved, the students achieved greater understanding and interpretation of the author's words.

One year, I invested just under forty dollars in a secondhand rug and couch for the purpose of reading (orally and silently). Results were better than I expected: A greater ability to focus, more comfort, very active discussions, significant enthusiastic participation.

The kids took turns sitting on the couch with the remainder of the group sitting or lying on the rug. It was different. It was enjoyable. As an example of its affect upon the classroom environment, I include the following experience that occurred recently:

I ran into Tammy and her dad in a nearby Walmart. She is now an adult in her late twenties. Within fifteen seconds of our conversation, she began to reminisce.

"Sixth grade was a lot of fun!"

"You remember what it was like?"

With an expression of searching memory, she replied, "I remember sitting on a couch or the carpet reading, *Are You There, God; It's Me, Margaret* by Judy Blume. We were all sitting around talking about the book…but it wasn't like school. It was more like kids just hanging around, talking and having fun just like we did when we were out of school…reading in your class was really enjoyable."

Encourage Active Student Involvement: Within a unique, comfortable environment, your students may additionally achieve security, reassurance, and motivation, which can usher in more active scholastic dialogue and progress.

A secure, relaxed setting more easily:

- Builds small group trust and support.

- Introduces a "group process" of working together.

- Increases awareness of self and others.

- Increases communication, active listening, and trust.

- Bridges gaps among genders, personalities, temperaments, etc.

- Involves everyone.

- Builds supportive groups to prevent aberrant behavior (loneliness, rejection, negative peer pressure, failure, tension).

- Inspires.

INVOLVE THEM...THEY WILL REMEMBER.

Additional suggestions:

- How about one or two students, with your guidance, taking a chunk of a future lesson and actually teaching it? Yes, they can! With a team approach and sufficient preparation time, a group can quite easily acquire a formidable comprehension of a topic. It will reinforce their knowledge, not to mention involving the rest of the class in a successfully unique and entertaining approach. The whole idea could academically motivate the other class members, especially if they, too, will be taking on a lesson responsibility.

- How about video-taping them as they teach, having the class view it, then perhaps, passing the recording on to other classrooms? Possibly devise other methods to involve them in an unconventional way.

- To back up my suggestion to totally involve your students in the lessons, I offer the following information regarding retention rates among students as they relate to Teaching Styles: Consider the Learning Pyramid, developed by The National Training Labs in Bethel, Maine.

WHERE ARE YOU AND YOUR STUDENTS FOUND ON THE LEARNING PYRAMID?

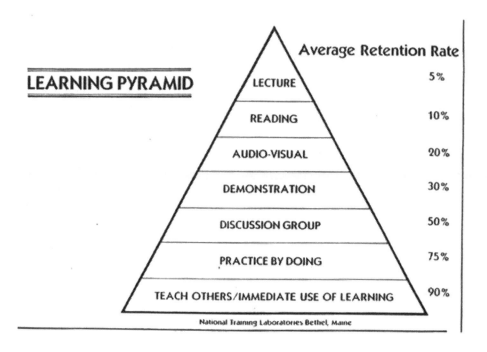

JOY OF TEACHING #4: SINCERE INFLUENCE AND CONCERN

Without warning, you notice that a working student appears troubled, stressed, anxious…. You approach her desk and speak to her softly offering helpful suggestions. Looking into her eyes and putting your hand tenderly on her shoulder you pause and conclude with, "I know you can do it." She smiles, glows a bit, then…she does it.

———

You spent extra time with him working over a mathematical problem, reconstructing a paragraph, or possibly explaining a class assignment. You were happy to do it; you felt helpful. Then, you went on about your business and focused upon it no longer. The next day, you spot him as the two of you pass in the corridor. You smile and say hello…he's looking at you differently, however. It's not just the smile or the stare,…it's that he obviously did not forget about the time you spent together.

———

You displayed reassuring comfort to her; a word of caution, perhaps… or plain, simple advice. The event concluded. She thanked you and moved on through the day, through the year, through her life. Will you remember the event in twenty or thirty years? Will she?

A few years ago, I'd stopped at a neighborhood pharmacy on my way home to make a small purchase. As I approached the cashier with my item, I overheard the words, "He was my favorite teacher." Out of the corner of my eye, I focused to my left, where I observed two women a short distance away staring at me. I recognized the red-headed young lady on the left as the name, "Vickie," quickly formed in my mind. A considerable amount of time had elapsed since I'd last seen her. However, I remembered her as a kind, sensitive, hard-working student who enjoyed attending class.

While continuing to observe me, she added, "He's the only teacher that really taught me something." At that point, there was no stopping me.... Walking up to the women, I acknowledged recognizing Vickie and asked how she was doing. Without hesitating for an instant, she briefly related the story of experiencing a social difficulty with several classmates while in sixth grade. She then, informed me that I'd had a conversation with her, giving her advice as to how to go about dealing with the challenge. As she described the event, my suggestion apparently had worked, and the problem was put to rest.

She'd married and had a son,... twenty years old! At the time, she was forty-two! Naturally, I didn't have the slightest idea as to the nature of the trouble she'd experienced thirty years prior, nor what advice I'd given her. However, the occurrence, once again, underscored my belief that teachers cannot be fully aware of their potential influence, nor to the length of time students remember their classroom encounters. I found it incredible and **so** emotionally moving.... You may not recall an event; but they surprisingly may.

JOY OF TEACHING #5: PLANTING SEEDS

I've enjoyed conversations with countless former students over the years. They are gratifying beyond description. It happens more frequently than it otherwise might because I still live in the same area where I taught. Consequently, I often meet many of the individuals that spent time in one of my classes. This, I believe, enables me to more frequently stir their memories and receive their sometimes-flattering comments.

How many seeds have you planted? How often have former students moved through their academic years into adulthood thinking of you or mentioning your name? How frequently did their thoughts flow back to an experience that they shared with you?

If you are unable to experience occasional meetings with them, you might not be aware of these pleasant memories. Rest assured, however; they did occur. Your students grow up, remembering.... They remember *you*. Think about it.

JOY OF TEACHING #6: NOSTALGIA

You come across a folder, booklet, file, or envelope containing mementos representing many of the wonderful things that happened to you during part of your career. As you peruse the contents, the memories come flooding back. You're still; you become a bit lost in an event that occurred years ago, your eyes blur...how wonderful is the nostalgic ecstasy. Keep the file safely set aside for those occasions when you have a tough day. Then seek the mementos again and feel comforted.

CHAPTER 3: A DAY TO REMEMBER

There will be no indication, no warning, that upon this day, an event will occur that you'll remember...forever....

The experience may most likely begin as any other teaching day... comments exchanged with colleagues in the corridor prior to class; last minute lesson changes; handout sheets prepared on your desk; materials arranged in appropriate locations; instructions written for pupils to copy....

But later, without warning, something evolves that makes the day totally exclusive. You will remember the look in her eyes, the sadness in his voice, the unexpected anger, the joy in her behavior, or the unforeseen tragic news that sadly reached your ears. How many have you experienced? If recently joining the ranks of educators, how many *will* you encounter? You'll never forget them.

INCIDENT #1: SANDY

It was the last day of my first year of teaching. I'd made all final preparations ...report cards piled on my desk, slips from the principal ready to be passed out, final comments memorized. There was more than the usual laughter and joy preceding the bell. With the loud familiar ring, all quieted down and waited. I passed out the necessary materials, made my last comments, and offered my wish for a happy summer and successful year in the seventh grade. I became silent; they stared. It was time to say good-bye. Though totally aware of the thoughts and feelings beginning to reach my mind, and my heart, I focused upon the necessity to maintain my composure. After all, I was the <u>teacher</u>, a role model. I did not want to come off as a strange emotional adult in those days. Once more, I waited for the bell.

It rang. "Good-bye, good-bye, have a great summer, do your best next year, good-bye, Tom; thank you, Denice; good-bye, Lisa…"

…Sandy didn't follow the rest of her class down the corridor. Remaining by the doorway, one hand locked around the elbow of the other arm, she stood staring into my eyes, her bottom lip beginning to quiver. Sandy had been raised by a single mom and genuinely warmed up to me over a very short time beginning early in the year. I stared at the young lady, having not the slightest idea what the problem was, nor what to do. After several extremely long seconds, she finally managed, "…I don't want to *leave*…," as tears welled up in her eyes. Following far too long a pause, I replied, "I'll miss you too, Sandy." I was lost, totally surprised, without direction…I had no idea what to say to her. She suddenly spun around and quickly made her way down the corridor.

I managed to find my way to my desk and simply sat staring at the floor. I'd failed to deal with the event successfully. It was my first year; I'd not hugged *one* kid between September and June. I had much to learn. The incident embedded itself in my mind. I've not forgotten one second of her departure.

Have you had a similar event?

INCIDENT #2: ANNIE

Two years later, it was Annie: same time of year, last day, everything completed. She'd been a shy, quiet young lady, who had moved to America from another country and consequently was having difficulty with the English language. She surprised me with her comment, stated with absolutely correct grammar and considerable volume…. "I will never forget you!…" A hug did occur to me, but by that time, she was scurrying down the hall on her way to the line of buses awaiting the kids for the last time that year. Next time, I would be prepared.

INCIDENT #3: RONALD

He was a quiet boy…few smiles, no laughter, serious in appearance. After observing him for several weeks, I'd concluded that the "serious" exterior was caused by the uncertainty as to his role in school,...as well as his role in life.

When called upon, there were times when he would simply sit, uncomfortably rolling to his hip, staring at his desk, and not utter a single word. He often did not know the answer; he often did not complete his homework...so frequently, in fact, I concluded that a home visit was necessary. I wished to make certain that he had a time scheduled for homework, that all necessary materials were available on his desk or table, and that there was suitable room for all his books in order to make the nightly routine easier and more comfortable for him. ...I was in for quite a surprise.

I'd not yet visited one home within the first year of my career. His would be the first. A few days before the scheduled visit, I was approached by Mary, the school nurse and long- time veteran of the system. She was a seasoned, extremely confident, and capable woman.

"I hear that you're making a home visit to the Benford home."

"Yes, on Thursday. Why?"

"I'll go with you."

"You don't have to go with me, Mary."

"You've never been there before, right?"

"No, I haven't. Why?"

"I'll go with you." And she continued moving down the hall.

We rode together, that Thursday, in her car.

My first surprise was the condition of the home's exterior. Paint peeling, broken window frames, missing handrail, steps requiring attention, lawn area with no grass whatsoever. Mary's knock on the door was followed by the piercing response, "Come in!"

The door knob continued to spin as she attempted to enter. Finally, someone opened the door from the inside. It was Ronald's mom...looking disheveled, unprepared, uncomfortable...hair unattended, barefoot, and wearing an old, poorly fitting, long black dress with white trim. The woman asked why we'd scheduled the visit. I had to totally concentrate on her question, as she had only a few teeth, and her words were a bit difficult to interpret.

I began to explain my concern. As I spoke, I noticed the room was lit by a bare, dusty, cobweb-covered light bulb, mid-ceiling. The dishes in the sink and on the counter, were attended by hovering flies, obviously having been there for days. Dilapidated furniture was scattered around the home, and everything was in disarray.

Eventually, the dad entered the room and angrily joined the conversation…however, I could not understand him. I never truly comprehended his difficulty in making his words clear; it appeared that his struggle to communicate arose from some type of speech problem. His wife attempted to explain what he was saying, but made little progress.

I was stunned. This was where Ronald lived, where he existed, his family, his home, his world. Instead of making suggestions as to how he could more successfully take on the challenge of homework, I stared around the room attempting to interpret the world within which this kid survived. There was no desk, no table at which he could complete his assignments. I was totally unprepared for the encounter. Mary took over. She appealed to the parents to enforce some type of homework supervision, and we left.

I felt hopeless, unable to offer a single suggestion. I'd never seen anything like it. In checking his attendance record, I saw that he had extremely few absences. For the first time in my career, I concluded that a student of mine attended school on a daily basis simply because he preferred our building over the environment of his family's home. Sadly, there would be numerous future occasions in my career when I would reach the same conclusion with other students. The fact that Ronald was not making much academic progress did not affect his daily appearances. Mary said, "Tell me if you want to visit another time. I'll go with you." We never returned.

While Ronald was in my class, I was taking a course on adolescent psychology. The instructor was a college professor as well as a well-seasoned, experienced clinical psychologist who treated countless youngsters. I decided to show the instructor a picture that Ronald had drawn and given to me. I located the drawing of a boy dark, gloomy, and depressing in structure and color, and I wondered if he might venture a comment about my student based upon the picture. He did: "This boy is lost. He is unhappy and feels totally alone as though he has no one to rely upon." It certainly made sense.

A few weeks later, I asked Ronald to help me clean my parents' cellar (it was my second year of teaching, and I was still living with my mom and dad a short distance from the school).

I told him that it needed some cleaning and a number of objects were to be moved. I insisted that he accept payment for the work even though it appeared that the visit to my home was already enough to positively motivate him. As far as the job we hired him to complete, it was non-existent. I'd created a myth. I felt that, perhaps, after finishing the work, he would have a chance to experience some pride in the successful accomplishment of a task, not to mention the pleasure of earning a few dollars, as well.

We spent an hour or so in the cellar, with me telling him what to move or where to sweep. Then I paid him. Following that, I explained that we were well into dinnertime and he might as well take part in our meal. Mom had everything on the table, and I explained that I just didn't want to take the time to run him home while letting the food get cold, so he might as well join the family. He eagerly agreed.

Ronald consumed more than a considerable amount of food. When he stood up from the table, his stomach protruded to such an extent over his belt, I became a bit concerned...would he experience some kind of digestive difficulty? Fortunately, when he came into class on the following day, he appeared fine. The entire episode seemed to dissolve some of his discomfort when around me. Academically, however, he continued to experience considerable difficulty.

I never got over the home visit. It educated me, unfortunately, in learning a challenging lesson. The teacher can never fully anticipate what to expect of a student's home environment, nor what effect it may be having on the youngster and his view of the world. This boy's early life struggle still weighs upon me, even though I know he eventually moved out of the home, found a job, got married, and had a daughter. Yeah, he did...many years later, she was in my class, as well.

INCIDENT #4: THE SEAT OF DISTINCTION

My class had been involved in this unique activity that promotes communication, peer acceptance, and bonding while discouraging injury to classmates' pride and self-criticism. The key facet of the lesson was allowing classmates to deliver sincere complimentary messages to each individual sitting in The Seat of Distinction. Responses from those occupying the chair were limited to the simple words, "Thank you." The session had gone on for over half the period. As the last student to receive positive comments rose to his feet, Amanda began asking me quite loudly why I hadn't taken a turn sitting in "The Chair." I politely refused, but then heard the voices of nearly every kid in the room joining in the effort. So,...I consented. I needed to display my respect for the activity, showing them how much I thought of the whole idea, myself.

As usual, my eye was on the clock; I had several things I needed to cover before the bell screamed an end to the period. Consequently, I wished to occupy "The Seat," experience the "compliments," then move on to the next component of my lesson. Gradually, however, their comments drew my undivided attention; what transpired was unexpected. I can recall the following comments:

"Mr. Sgambato, you always know what we're thinking."

"Mr. Sgambato, you discipline us without yelling. You talk to us."

"Mr. Sgambato, you're organized."

"Mr. Sgambato, you read out loud—like, with feeling."

"Mr. Sgambato, you're my favorite, all-time teacher."

"Mr. Sgambato, I wish you could always be my teacher, through twelfth grade."

"Mr. Sgambato, I didn't like language arts before this year. Now, I love it."

"Mr. Sgambato, I didn't like writing till this year."

"Mr. Sgambato, you have ESP."

"Mr. Sgambato, you're funny!"

"Mr. Sgambato, you make us laugh."

"Mr. Sgambato, you're not like most other teachers."

At that point, I found it quite difficult recalling my plans for the remainder of the lesson...that I'd found so compelling before occupying the "Seat of Distinction."

I'm pretty sure I postponed them until the next day;...not really certain; I don't remember...thanks to Amanda.... Had it not been for her determination to get the teacher into The Seat, I'd never have heard the wonderful comments made by my students.

Now, we must keep in mind, of course, that opinions concerning their teacher could easily have changed by the following year, the following week, or even later the same day. Nevertheless, the compliments did, in fact, prove that, at that time, I was contributing to their educational comfort and progress. I was making a *difference*.

I'm not suggesting that you necessarily introduce, The Seat of Distinction, though instructions for it can be found later in this book. I'm pointing out that without such occasions, your students may lack the opportunities to deliver similar messages to their teacher.... However, it doesn't mean that the positive, thankful sentiments do not exist within them. They simply haven't been verbalized.

INCIDENT #5: KERRY

In one of my classroom approaches, I'd assigned The Sad Piece as a project for my language arts class. This was something I'd done every year following a string of lessons dealing with appropriate, feeling words, applicable adjectives, to be used in composing. Instructions were to use accurate and suitable adjectives, adverbs, and verbs that would allow the reader of the piece to experience some of the same feelings the author had encountered during an actual sad event in his or her life.

I'd had the sincere pleasure that year of instructing a very bright, totally academically devoted young lady by the name of Kerry in my class. She was out in front, eager to learn, and happy to please. Approximately three weeks prior to this assignment, a tragedy had sadly occurred in Kerry's life; her father had taken his own life. The event affected everyone that knew this young lady. She managed, but the experience most certainly was terribly distressing.

It occurred to me that she might attempt to use the event as the basis for the assignment; I waited and watched. When word reached me that she was indeed pursuing the incident as the basis for her Sad Piece, I called her mother. Her mom and I shared the same opinion: She was a talented, confident, intelligent girl. We both felt that not only was she capable of dealing with the event, but it might also help her to successfully manage her emotions if she could express her feelings on paper.

After several days of writing, editing, and rewriting, members of the class were taking turns reading their Sad Pieces to the entire group. Kerry raised her hand. I chose another student. She was determined, continuously raising her hand while staring into my eyes. After ignoring her for the third time, I felt that my intentions were becoming obvious. I called on her to share her paper. As she walked toward the front of the room, she giggled a bit. During the first few paragraphs, she smiled and laughed again several times while delivering passage after passage of serious, heartbreaking accounts of the occurrence. She was attempting, I believe, to embrace the opposite emotion from that which she truly felt. She'd chosen to avoid revealing the emotional reaction expected by her classmates. As Kerry continued reading, smiling, and giggling, I didn't totally understand, but felt that I should intervene. I slowly made my way to her side; she continued reading and chuckling. I placed my hand on her shoulder. She stopped reading, dropped her hands to her sides, and stared at the class. Suddenly, she spun to me sobbing, and hastily wrapped her arms around my waist, squeezing,…. All of her classmates were understandably affected,… some of them crying, as well. Her body shook as she wept. I pulled her to me and did not speak a word; I simply waited. She did not need some adult telling her that things would be all right. Things were not all right, and it would be a long time before she might regain her characteristic joyful personality. Following the event, I engaged in several more conversations with Kerry and with her mother…I sadly remember.…

INCIDENT #6: A VISIT

Between lunch and fifth period, one afternoon, I received a visit from Cheryl. At the time, she was a high school senior living in Florida and visiting her home town of Fort Plain, New York. Even with all that time having gone by, she retained the same smiling, pleasant attitude, bubbling with enthusiasm and sincerity.

"The room looks different, smaller, but I remember it. I remember lots of the stuff that you did. I don't remember any of my other classes, but I remember yours."

So few words can mean so much. It made my day. What if she'd not visited? I'd never have had the opportunity to enjoy her words.

INCIDENT #7: MARK

This young man was well behaved. He listened in class and often raised his hand to participate. If his answer was not correct, it didn't stop him from raising his hand again moments later. Mark lived on a farm with his grandparents, enthusiastically helping them to operate it on a daily basis. At a point during the year, both grandparents became ill. Mark had no choice; he took over *every* responsibility on the farm...including early milking. Remember, this kid was twelve years old.

Surprisingly, he missed no days of school during this period of nearly two weeks. This student displayed a remarkable sense of control and effort. He did what he recognized as *the right thing,*... and he never once complained. His grandparents had raised him well. While watching a video in class, during that two weeks, one of the students reported to me, "Mr. Sgambato, Mark is sleeping."

I replied, "Yes, I know; shhh."

INCIDENT #8: JANIE

I spotted Janie walking toward us as her teacher and I chatted. She was an eleven-year-old special education student, and though I never had her in one of my classes, we'd struck up several conversations over the earlier months of school. She had an active sense of humor, which I enjoyed stimulating. We'd enjoyably developed a relationship. There were, however, aspects of her life of which I was unaware.

As she neared us, she smiled and said, "Hi, Mr. Funny" (her original name for me). This young lady had such a pleasing smile and remained incredibly likable. I replied, "Hi, Janie!".... Then humorously added, "Hey, why don't you come live with me; I've got a real strange dog you'd like named Juan. We could play hide-and-seek with him."

"I'd like that!" she replied. Then, with a rather serious expression, she quickly walked off. The reply was unexpected and left me a bit confused. It was then that her teacher explained: Janie lived with a foster family that cared for a total of three of our school's students. They recently decided to adopt two of the kids; Janie was not one of them. I had had no idea.... The rest of my day seriously lacked luster....

INCIDENT #9: GREG

I moved my eyes slowly from left to right, row to row, student to student. All faces were totally unfamiliar to me. It was their first day in my sixth-grade classroom. One of the new students, Greg, obviously avoiding eye contact, appeared quiet and shy...not necessarily unusual for the beginning of the school year.

On the following afternoon, I stood in the doorway welcoming students as they entered the room again. The closer he got to me, the less frequently he raised his eyes. By the time he was directly in front of me, he was staring at the floor with head tipped slightly to one side. During the following days, whenever I noticed this young man walking through the corridor from one class to another, he was always alone...quiet, wearing a backpack, head tipped, hands in his pockets. He had no siblings,... nor did he retain any visible friends, despite having attended our school since kindergarten. His classmates did not relate to him at all. From an administrative professional, I'd been given the information that "...things were not the best with this young man." I could only guess what that meant. My presumption was that he had a feeling of inferiority, possibly caused by treatment and comments heard on a daily basis.

In class, he sat slouched in his seat occasionally raising his eyes, but not enthusiastically involved. There were times, of course, when I simply called on him, hand raised or not. He would respond in a low, unsteady voice. On occasion, his reply would be correct. More often, it was not.

I took it upon myself to offer some of my attention, energy, and humor during informal occasions. Behind the quiet, reluctant surface, a reflection of gratitude sometimes appeared. He'd smiled...I'd made progress. I was happy.

I knew enough not to apply too many humorous approaches as it might imply greater attention, producing the opposite result from that which I was seeking. Additionally, I avoided small audiences during the encounters. I knew I'd have more success dealing with him one on one.

Time moved on. After several months, he appeared to become a bit more comfortable within the classroom environment. When he laughed at my comments, he was able to maintain eye contact. A noticeable improvement...great! During the remainder of the days, however, he continued to appear depressed, despondent.

One evening, following dinner, the phone rang. The words of the caller embedded themselves in my mind:

"Mr. Sgambato, this is Sheriff Ensun. Did you have a student by the name of Greg Ellington?"

I was an English teacher, very much aware of past and present verb tenses. The caller had used the verb **"did."** It indicated that something was now in the past. I quickly told myself that Greg's family had possibly moved away because of legal difficulties, or that he'd simply been taken out of my class. I strongly attempted to ignore any other possibility and need for the use of the past-tense verb, "did."

I paused. The sheriff waited for my reply. After what seemed like minutes, I said, "Yes, why?"

"...Well...I'm afraid he's dead."

I felt myself go into some kind of "automatic mode." I stepped away from my feelings as best I could. My greatest fear had come to pass. "How did he die?" I managed.

"Well...he shot himself with a shotgun."

The force of my emotions urged me to end the call. I held on in order to answer the sheriff's questions about my possibly noticing any recent changes in Greg's behavior. I described the kind of boy I'd observed him to be. Then, after thanking me, the sheriff was off the line. I succumbed to my feelings for a rather lengthy time, then simply sat and stared without moving. Though I pleaded with myself to sadly accept the incident and not become overwhelmed emotionally, the question weighed on my mind... how could *I* have allowed this to happen. He'd spent time under *my* control. *I* possessed skills...the skills to bring him a bit of contentment, humor, self-esteem. Why had *I* not seen this coming? How much of the blame was my own? I suppose these types of thoughts and feelings are understandable for an individual who spends a quantity of hours dealing with adolescents, then faces such a horrific event as this. It was devastating.

On the following morning, I took it upon myself to inform the class. I had to take some action. I could not allow them to be informed by word of mouth through the course of the day. Someone had to take the time,... quality time, to explain, inform, allow questions, allow mourning, silence, and tears.... I'd never expected, as a teacher, to be confronted with the agony of this terrible manner of human loss. I pleaded with God not to ever have it happen again...but it did...three more times....

INCIDENT #10: DON

Teachers can be easily surprised and sometimes even shocked as to what is taking place in a student's life without our knowledge. Don,... what a kid!...intelligent, thoughtful, sensitive, and quiet. At the beginning of the year, I initiated a lesson in which class members responded to a collection of questions I'd devised to help us know each other better. One of the questions on the form asked, "If you could have three wishes, what would they be?"

During a class discussion based upon the questions, Don raised his hand, "I only have one wish. I wish my mother would come back home." There followed a lengthy moment of silence. All were still. He then continued to work his way through the remainder of questions with no further reference to his one wish. I found it difficult to concentrate for a few seconds. I was aware of the parents' separation, yet had seen no reaction to the estrangement up to that point. I kept a closer eye upon him following that lesson.

About half way through the year, I noticed that Don was using two book bags to transport his school materials from room to room. This observation reinforced my concern that we might be inconveniencing our students by asking them to carry around so many books for the five subjects taking place within the longer second part of the school day.

As it turned out, Don's decision to use two book bags had nothing to do with the number of afternoon courses he was taking. When I asked about the bags, he responded that each of his parents had given him one. At all costs, he explained, it was paramount that he not slight either parent by using only one of the gifts. I totally understood, but, unfortunately, I remained helpless in resolving his dilemma.

INCIDENT #11: SUPPORT GROUP

I strongly believe that today's students should have access to support groups. The concept introduces the kids to a setting within which they can begin interacting, building trust, as well as self-respect in a sheltered environment. By expressing inner feelings about almost anything, they see that other adolescents often have many of the same concerns they do. Additionally, they readily receive feedback about their problems, and become less apprehensive about what they may perceive as their own shortcomings.

Several months before I retired from teaching, I'd activated the very last support group I'd facilitate, and was anxious to begin the first session. Permission slips from parents had been returned, a time and place had been arranged, and all had gathered for the initial experience. After an appropriate welcoming, followed by comments describing member responsibilities and confidentiality, two members apparently felt comfortable enough to engage in self-revelation. I was extremely pleased that the members took on the responsibilities so quickly and comfortably. Everyone participated.

The second session, two days later, was even more successful. One student eloquently and honestly described exactly how she felt and what she'd determined was responsible for her emotional state. Others responded quickly and sincerely in very supportive fashion. Empathy was displayed and tears were thereafter shed. The session was unexpectedly very moving for one and all. Parents would have been surprised and impressed. The problem wasn't totally solved, but excellent progress was made. Everyone left the room feeling better and perhaps even a bit grateful for the experience,…especially the facilitator.

INCIDENT #12: CAROL

Occasionally, Carol wouldn't have her homework completed. She was such a good kid; why no homework? I'd scolded her from time to time. However, on one particular day, I felt a need to slow down and ease off a bit. She looked exhausted. I approached, took her hand, and pulled her out of her seat and into the hall for a short walk.

Putting my arm around her shoulder, I said, "Carol, whenever I have to scold you for not having your homework done, it hurts me." We'd stopped walking; she stared at me, blinking. "I do not enjoy scolding you. I like you. What's going on?"

She replied, "We had our house inspection, and I had to help clean it."

"How long did it take to clean?

"We didn't get the call until supper time."

"How long did you work?"

"I'm not sure; until after 9:00."

In class, we were working on possessive nouns…which are, indeed, important. We use them daily in our conversations and almost every time we lay pen to paper. Carol, however, had issues far overshadowing the importance of an English lesson and with which I've never had to deal. Should I have given her a detention,…scolded her in front of her peers, called home and complained to her parents that she'd not completed her homework on possessive nouns?

Gently, I pulled her head very close to my shoulder, and rubbing her arm, said, "Next time call me…and I'll help you deal with it." When I moved away from her, she was crying… arms hanging loosely by her sides, shoulders shaking with each whimper, not one attempt to cover her eyes, nor wipe the tears. She did not deserve such sadness…especially after putting in an entire school day despite the overwhelming fatigue.

"For a girl as wonderful as you, Carol, life will improve; not tonight, not next week,…perhaps not even next year. Eventually, it will be good. Be patient and do your best. If you'd like to go into the girls' room for a break, fine. I'll see you back in the room when you're ready." Sadly, I walked slowly toward the door to my room, unable to provide everything she needed; I was only her teacher. She needed so much more….

On the following day, I suggested joining our Support Group.

INCIDENT #13: THE TEACHER

It was the last week of the school year…as well as the last week of my teaching career. My decision to retire was based solely upon financial concerns rather than my physical or emotional needs.

Early in the period, I read my "Farewell" piece to the class. We'd formed a seated circle in fourth period, and I shared my very personal comments about leaving my teaching career. They knew me well, and I withheld nothing concerning my enjoyment of teaching and my sad reluctance to leave.

When I finished reading, all were very quiet; there was no movement by anyone. Jocelyn's head was uncharacteristically tipped to the side, hands tucked under her legs, eyes cast downward. Chris bent forward from his hips, eyes repeatedly moving from me to the floor…Jan's complexion changing as I looked at her, Jaime with tears in her eyes. Most were very still, eyes seeking to understand, possibly to comfort.

We sat like that for nearly an entire minute. Though tears began, heads remained still with eyes steadily upon me. I was surprised; my piece had moved them. Though somewhat appreciative that they thought that much of their teacher's predicament, I experienced guilt over the somber mood that I'd brought about. I'd made my students cry. It was not my intention. I passed out tissues. The boys, of course, weren't sure if they should openly accept a tissue or not…most surprisingly did. We continued to wait in silence as I leaned upon my podium, debating my next step.

Over the course of the year, they'd become aware of the strangeness of their teacher. However, they never anticipated my next move,... nor did I. A thought occurred to me. Without hesitation, I reached into the closet and pulled out my guitar. Along with it, I grabbed two tambourines, four maracas, and two claves to pass out. I can still recall their stares. (*Mr. Sgambato is doing it again...he is truly weird.*)

Over the next ten or so minutes, I proceeded to teach them lyrics of the song, "Come a Little Bit Closer," by Jay and the Americans; for those of you unfamiliar with the melody, it is *not* a somber tune. After assigning "instrumental parts," we went "on tour." We moved, through the corridors, from classroom door to classroom door, even into the main office—singing, entertaining. Everyone was kind enough to listen and applaud. It went so well. Tears were replaced by smiles...I was so proud....

The period ended. I quietly stood mid-corridor, guitar hanging on my side, slowly waving. They began to make their way to their next class... heads turned to me.... My students, staring and smiling as they walked away. I'd been so damn fortunate. In forty-five minutes, we'd experienced both ends of the emotional spectrum. I then went to lunch, **feeling....**

INCIDENT #14: YEAR'S END

2:20 p.m. End of the year. End of my career. Twenty-two of them sitting in front of me, talking, chuckling, waiting for their report cards. All very much aware of my limited time to be spent in the classroom.

I began handing them out. During the next few minutes, several handed me farewell notes or small departing gifts. The notes and gifts were, of course, prized possessions, my last ever to be received from students. Following the piercing ring of the bell, all left, making their way down the corridor for the last time that year.

I remained in the room, unable to leave. A colleague entered and asked, "Are you crying?" She gave me a hug, then went on her way.

I stared at the blank walls for a few seconds...until Kieren, Jan, Sara, Erin, and Chris stopped in. They noticed the drying tears, I'm sure. They thanked me for being their teacher and bade me good-bye. A few minutes later, Kieren returned, crying. My fault.

Hearing more footsteps, I looked up. Into the room, again marched Sara, Jan, Eric, and Chris. They stood staring at the floor, the wall. Silence permeated the room. Sara, with lips pursed, displayed an expression of concern and compassion as she briefly stared into my eyes. Suddenly, she broke the stillness by loudly proclaiming, "I want to swim in your pool!" The others nodded, chuckled, and expressed vocal agreement. I responded, "Of course," certain that they would never actually do so. She, then, chose a date...July 13, to which I agreed. Her words and volume didn't seem to match her mood. I began to slowly understand. She was not doing this for herself.

They each approached for a hug and departed. With tears returning, I was alone once more. The remainder of the brief day was quiet, lonely, emotional....

Carrying my last few materials out of the room, I stopped at the door one last time. I began to survey the empty walls, desks, and chairs,...as I recalled the hands in the air, the excitement, the laughter, the immeasurable pleasures of teaching...hundreds of students,...thousands....

I then turned off the lights;...darkness...the last chapter came to an end.

On July 13, they all arrived,...on time,...with bathing suits. I got to see them one more time. They swam in my pool. They swam in *my* pool.... Maybe Sara simply enjoyed swimming in pools?

No, I don't believe so.

CHAPTER 4: FELLOWSHIP; THE FEEL OF SUPPORT

Arrive to school by 7:45. Work at your profession and get the job done. Leave no later than 3:30. As you walk down the corridor, bid your good-byes. "See you Monday."

Anything missing?

How well do you know your colleagues? Is it important for you to truly *know* them? Do you gather? (Now, what's the author suggesting?) How could teachers ever find time to *gather*? They have enough to do. And besides, they work together professionally; it isn't as though they have to be buddies, right? Please keep reading....

When teachers who are educational colleagues take the opportunity to enhance relationships, I believe that they cannot help benefiting. They come to better know each other both professionally and personally. In Fort Plain, N.Y., there was no deliberate effort to bring about camaraderie, fellowship, or personal encouragement among colleqgues. No one designed a plan aimed at developing a system of support and companionship for our teachers. Somewhere along the line, we simply found that we enjoyed each other's company, and sometimes needed a friend nearby to listen to our stories and concerns, or perhaps provide recommendations and assistance regarding student needs. Personal advice and support were always available. A pleasant reality indeed existed.

Watching Mr. Gifford demonstrate, to twenty-four focused eighth-graders, the proper way to kick a field goal summoned my respect for his patience and *professional experience*. On another occasion, while sitting in his home, I listened to his advice regarding my difficulty in facing a divorce. Not only did I admire his professional approaches to the art of teaching physical education; his personal help and attention summoned my gratitude for his personal friendship as well.

Mr. Ethington was able to prepare a dynamite introduction to the study of Ancient Egypt; talented man. He was also present at the service for my departed father, offering condolence, support, and companionship.

Taking notes as Mr. Murray explained a new classroom approach for team-building created a feeling of creative pleasure within me. He was a true professional with keen student perception and professional understanding. Between classes, we spent considerable time together sharing remarkable stories about so many wonderful youngsters. Truly, a rewarding personal relationship.

Admittedly, the further one travels to work, the less likely one is to spend additional time in the school building after hours. The rewards obtained, however, often make the expenditure of time well worth the investment.

During much of my career, the year began with a picnic attended by all. I might have found myself sitting at a table with a couple of "kitchen ladies," three or four teachers, a custodian, the superintendent, and all their family members. What did we discuss? *Anything!* We became better acquainted and less likely to remain among "our own kind." All were important supporters of a school system, and this comingling was an important factor in our working together, supporting each other, and striving for excellence. Who benefited?...everyone, especially the students. No matter what the kids' needs were, frequent positive interaction among the entire staff made the deliverance of those necessities that much more likely and with greater haste.

Additionally, when Friday arrived, it frequently meant a gathering, whether at the Charter House, The Old Mill Inn, or perhaps a colleague's home. These get-togethers provided enjoyment, laughter, relaxation, and, intuitively, *team building.*

The Christmas break often began with a party at the home of the principal, followed the same week with a party at a neighborhood restaurant.

On several Friday afternoons during the year, we gathered at the home of the head custodian for card games, bocce contests, horseshoes, beer, soda, barbecued chicken, and long periods of laughter. Did everyone always attend these events? If family responsibilities or a second income obligation intervened, we all understood because most of us had experienced them. However, just because the end of a school day arrived, it didn't mean that the relationships concluded.

The transition from professional to casual acquaintance proved to be a rewarding experience. Sharing time, backgrounds, goals, cocktails, and especially laughter expose participants to other dimensions of their colleagues' personalities. Stronger connections transpire. And, even if we don't always agree on topics pursued, we advance as professionals, individuals, and as a faculty. There is a greater tendency for the group to move forward together, arms interlocked, focused upon the same goal. Though we may have developed different teaching styles, they could be placed aside when it came time for more important educational pursuits. Yes, we were teachers; we were also, however, well acquainted, and consequently, many of us had become friends... and friends we remain.

I tell you of these occurrences not to persuade you to take the lead in necessarily organizing a "bonding event" (though that would certainly be fine); I simply wish you to remain *open* to the possibility of these types of activities occurring and consider my advice when I say that these endeavors are professionally helpful as well as immensely enjoyable.

ADMINISTRATORS

Did administrators attend our gatherings? There were some who felt, perhaps, a need to keep themselves separate from the masses (at least that was my perception) and consequently did not get involved. However, many of our principals and superintendents absolutely *did* frequently participate. I perceived that those events did, in fact, bring us closer together. Those who did not become involved most certainly did miss out.

Want to get to know the boss? Buy him a beer, or buy her a margarita. Then, sit and chat. And be yourself! Do not, for any reason, modify your personality, or purposely bring up serious school concerns during casual events. It is important that you remain true to your professional beliefs and to the person you truly are.

Now, what can we expect from administrators?

- They are all cut from the same mold.

- They're only interested in their own futures.

- All are politically motivated for selfish gains.

Yes, I did hear these accusations from time to time over my thirty-five years in education. And, yes—I did meet a few individuals who absolutely did fit some of the above descriptions. I also met a number of principals and superintendents who were dedicated, totally devoted to one thing: Improving the education of our system's students. When faced with a need to make a decision, their first consideration was how it would impact the student population rather than how it might affect their own career. Furthermore, they were not primarily interested in receiving gratitude or attention from the teachers, the board of education, or parents for putting in the time and work to achieve the objective. They did it because it served the needs of the school system. They were not interested in appearing *above* teachers; they stood side by side with us, arms interlocked with ours as we moved in the same direction. They worked with us, supported us, and strove for excellence. It was a pleasure.

———

He was in his office before I arrived; he was usually there at the end of the day as I left the building. He found a way to stimulate teachers; he encouraged them to continue working diligently for the improvement of our system of education...not to give up...and to remain hopeful and optimistic.

This man was the *best*,...none better. He made his decisions based solely upon the needs of the students. And, his door was always open...Hear what I'm saying...<u>always</u>! **<u>Thank you, Walt</u>**

SECTION TWO:

PROFESSIONAL ADVICE IN DEALING WITH YOUR STUDENTS

CHAPTER 5: LEARNING FROM EXPERIENCE

Four years of college, education courses, observations, student teaching, Bachelor's degree in teaching! Perhaps even a Master's

Totally ready!

Well, maybe,...

...or maybe not....

What else could possibly help tailor a teacher's proficiency in the classroom?

The only thing missing, of course, is experiential wisdom... that which is learned through extensive classroom involvement. There are, obviously, no courses available. These are the skills usually acquired through years of "on-the job" encounters.

I believe, however, that this chapter may be of help.

Whether you're totally new to the classroom, or on-the-job for a number of years, consider, perhaps, the suggestions below. Ultimately, they may boost your skills and save you time.

LEARNING FROM EXPERIENCE #1: SUPPORT AND EMPATHY

Is a student apt to do better academically if she perceives your genuine concern for her welfare? No question; a teacher's sincerity and compassion are important tools of the trade. They don't need to be planned, prepared, and released...they do require, however, to be offered by the teacher and observed by the student. If you allow your desires of support and empathy to manifest, they can be perceived by your pupil. The youngster who is easily intimidated when called upon to answer questions or asked to participate in class needs to *feel* your encouragement through your demeanor, your eye contact, body language, nearness, choice of terminology, and sometimes, even gentleness.

Again, the instructor needn't "prepare" these behaviors. One must simply *permit* them to be expressed, to surface in one's approach. The message of patience, understanding, and concern is then conveyed. Once the student successfully interprets the teacher's willingness to help, she may be encouraged to try, to work harder, to maintain a higher level of attentiveness and energy in achieving success in the classroom. So, if you like kids and you love teaching, it's easy. Just be yourself; the kid will most likely sense your sincerity and kindness, grow in confidence, and give it her best.

LEARNING FROM EXPERIENCE #2: RESPECT

What are your feelings as you enter the classroom? Are you all business? Do you focus strongly on discipline? Do you enter the "world" of your students and engage? Is there time for humor in your lesson? Is *respect* important?

Respect for whom?

Am I talking about students' respect for the teacher or the teacher's respect for the students? The answer is "yes" to both.

A teacher once commented to me, "They *must* respect me; I am their teacher, an adult. If they want *my* respect, however, they must earn it." The attitude, I believe, is coarse, unrealistic, and self-defeating. Truthfully, many students won't remember the subject matter you taught. A few may even forget your particular grade level. Nearly all, however, will remember how you treated them, and what they *derived from the relationship*. Why not take advantage of your position to role-model respect? This would encourage the student to feel accepted, as though he/she will be treated fairly and honestly. And when many of these youngsters view respect displayed by the teacher, they are more inclined to incorporate the behavior within their own lives.

Remember, it is the environmentally comfortable student who is usually more willing to take on academic responsibilities throughout the year. Now, I'm not suggesting that your display of "respect" be exaggerated. Just be yourself. An amicable, respectful teacher, I believe, stands a greater chance of persuading young people to follow. Respect for students equates to an extended hand followed by the words, "Come with me upon this journey."

Some of the most important things we teach may be our intrinsic values. We don't have to put them into words. All we have to do is live them. We become living examples, hopefully displaying empathy, patience, respect, understanding, tolerance, dignity, and… a sense of humor. Without question, it's a presentation of your personal values that makes up a large part of what you'll be teaching your students.

LEARNING FROM EXPERIENCE – #3: DON'T LET THEM HIDE

You, no doubt, have already experienced it. Some young people attempt to hide behind averted glances or eyes that roll to the ceiling, even looks of defiance. They frequently feel a need to conceal their feelings, thoughts, or moods. Though they are unwilling to admit this, even to themselves, some are quite proficient in this behavior. However, if you move in closer to the individuals and offer a sincere, receptive expression, you may, nevertheless, succeed in capturing their attention. Consequently, they will have difficulty preventing you from reading their eyes. It isn't necessary to remain in close proximity for lengthy periods, only long enough to make an open, friendly offer. You'll know them better; they'll know you better.

LEARNING FROM EXPERIENCE #4: UNCONVENTIONAL DISCIPLINE AND SECOND ORDER CHANGE

"Stop that!" "Sit down!" "I said, sit down!" "Please keep quiet!" "Stop it!" "Stop it right now!" "I'm not going to tell you again!" "I said, sit down!" "I'm waiting!" "I'm not going to tell you again!"

These outbursts may work at first. Then, however, many students grow used to hearing the orders delivered in the same manner and consequently, may more easily ignore them. Many teachers, too often, continue using the same attempts at disciplining the kids. Result: Less and less effective, to say the least. That is a result of **First Order Change** (using the *same* unsuccessful methods in attempting to obtain *different* behavior). When attempting to affect students' conduct, while using First Order Change, one ends up doing and saying the same things over and over again. The result? Behavior is unchanged. That's because <u>the teacher's</u> behavior is unchanged.

In **Second Order Change**, the teacher alters what he/she says and does in order to strongly influence a change in behavior. The Philosophy: Do it differently...even be a bit unorthodox. Try not to use anger, threats, volume, or any other disengaging tactics.

My advice: Do not approach the arena of discipline in the manner *anticipated by the student*. Approach in a unique fashion. It saves time, works better, and avoids unpleasant results. I'll give you an idea as to what I'm suggesting:

One of the most successful obstructions in preventing a teacher's perceptive ability to read a student's true intention is the kid's "Anger Block." Now, you, of course, are the adult, the teacher, the one in charge. However, sometimes it's necessary for the teacher to step back, allowing the emotional situation to de-escalate. Be patient, allowing the state of affairs to settle a bit. Look for an opportunity, possibly a short time later, to approach the student in a mild manner to talk, clarify, and give him evidence that you are not his enemy. This could be done during study hall, after school, or even on an occasion where you've stepped into the corridor to engage in a conversation concerning his disruptive behavior, demand for attention, or intrusion upon the teacher's class time. The trip into the corridor, though not the most ideal tactic to employ, may be, on occasion, the only recourse available. It may have been apparent to the entire class, of course, that he's *misbehaved*, he's *wrong*. His response to your "invitation" to leave the classroom for a chat was a shaking of his head, perhaps, a hard push on the desk in sliding his chair back, and a defiant glare in his eyes.

Once in the hall, he's expecting your demeaning words, your volume, your criticism—First Order Change. Instead of immediately scolding him through your own expression of anger, how about beginning slowly, with something unexpected, like, "Your two buddies, Frankie and Peter, must think that I'm yelling at you. Yep, I can see them staring at the door, nodding with expressions of certainty." His defiant glare may not melt away, but don't let that stop you. He most likely is trying to figure out what is happening. Meanwhile, his anger may be unexpectedly taking a "back seat" (de-escalation is beginning to occur).

At that point, with non-threatening body posture and volume, proceed to explain to him, from an honest, personal point of view, why you need everyone's attention. What he's doing is costing you time...and once the time is lost, you usually can't make it up. Though you know of everyone's need for attention, loss of class time is unfair to *all* the students in the class as well as to you; *you* are the teacher, with the responsibility to *Teach*. Your obligation is important. Engage his eyes and explain it in your own manner, possibly in a softer tone.

Though he may retain a look of anger, his brain may have begun to view his teacher in a totally new and unexpected way. He sees, perhaps more of who you truly are. You spoke to him firmly but with honesty, patience, and even a bit of respect. He may not easily forget this engagement. Believe me, you could very well be making a unique and lasting impression.

Then, to top it off, why not ask if he'd like to slowly walk by the door window to check out Frankie and Peter's behavior. Just as he begins to move, however, say, "Whatever you do, don't smile." This adds a touch of humor, but more importantly, an offer to *share* the moment, ridding the scene of a "teacher reprimanding student" theme. Following that, continue the discussion, seeking to determine if he truly understands your genuine intention. Now, do you actually have the time and freedom to step into the hall? It depends, of course, on the circumstances. Keep in mind that most of this scene could very well take place at the end of the school day, in private.

Will this always work? Perhaps not. (Would you be satisfied if it worked most of the time?) Can you use it with every student? In each case, you would have to be the judge. At times, you will need to rely on more conventional teacher-type responses. However, if possible:

- Allow de-escalation of emotion to take place, and...

- Employ an unorthodox approach when necessary; it gets their attention more easily and has greater potential of retaining their cooperation.

Misbehavior is not restricted only to boys; girls may participate, as well. In each of my examples, however, I will often refrain from using both male-female pronouns "he/she" on every occasion simply for reasons of reading simplicity.

To keep in mind: During adolescence, kids begin experiencing unfamiliar changes in their bodies **and** in their feelings. Many sense an impression of being misunderstood as they struggle out of childhood and into the world of adults. While attempting to wriggle free of their juvenile existence, they often exhibit defiant behaviors... disobedience, disrespect, sibling rivalry, lying, cheating, academic problems, negative attitudes, peer pressure, depression, and sexuality issues. Teachers need to keep this in mind when dealing with them.

Got a kid staying "after school?" Will you sit behind your desk working, as your pupil quietly sits, waiting to be dismissed, or will you consider the time an opportunity to make progress in helping him view the classroom differently and obtaining his cooperation? How can this youngster be approached in a way that will harness his attention, promote discussion, provide an opportunity for him to perceive your sincere concern and see you as a person with his best situation in mind? Remove the barrier! Grab a chair (not too close; don't intimidate), and start to pursue a dialogue.

POSSIBLE CONVERSATION STARTERS:

- "Steve, didn't I see you at last Friday's game? Did the score surprise you?"

- "Steve, what would you be doing if you weren't here?"

- "What is the worst part about our school?"

- "What is the best part about our school?"

The answer may very well be, "The bell at the end of eighth period." Fine, don't criticize his responses; ask *why?* Continue with conversation. Additional suggestions for initiating conversation are below:

- "What do you see yourself doing ten years from today?"

- "What is the best thing that could happen to you?"

- "If you could change one thing about our school, what would it be?"

- "How would you change it?"

- "If you could change one thing about yourself, what would it be?"

Just start it. Get a conversation going. You don't have to have a secure, detailed plan. Read the kid's mind a bit. Think back: Who are his friends? What types of behavior does he find amusing? What does his T-shirt say? Does it state the name of a band or sports team? Are you familiar with it? Use this information to your advantage.

There are times when a seemingly insignificant exchange or engagement occurs between teacher and student that redirects the relationship in a new and positive way.

Tom was a youngster I'd often noticed engaging enthusiastically with his rather active group of friends. While he was participating in their antics, I'd frequently witnessed his excellent sense of humor and bursts of contagious laughter. He totally enjoyed unconventional humor.

One day in the early part of the morning, for some reason, he'd stated loudly and angrily that he thought homework was "stupid" and actually walked out of the room just before the beginning of class, slamming the door behind him. After allowing as much time as possible for *de-escalation,* I slowly approached him in the hall. I then explained in a non-threatening but firm manner that he needed to spend some time with me at the end of the day.

Following the last class of the afternoon, he appeared at my door, then heaved his body into a chair. He'd been sitting in my room for about fifteen minutes pretending to read a novel while "staying after school." As he was engaged in staring at the book and doing nothing, I slyly pulled a tennis ball out of my desk and threw it toward the back of the room. I then quickly resumed working in my plan book. As the ball slammed against the closet door, he was startled, then looked at me with a blank stare for two seconds. He spun his head around to see where the ball had landed, then whirled around to me again. I stared at him, raised and lowered my eyebrows quickly, then returned my focus to my desk. The next thing I knew, he began to laugh almost uncontrollably. He had just witnessed a dimension of his teacher's unorthodox personality that he didn't know existed. He reacted, however, as he usually did to unconventional behavior... with laughter! This little nutty thing started it.

"You thought that was funny, didn't you?"

"Yeah..."

"Good, so did I. Not everyone does, you know (quick nods of agreement). Sometimes I get a little tired of being serious and feel like laughing.

You ever feel that way?" And so the conversation went, until I ended it with:

"Here's my message, Tom. Something was obviously bothering you. Was it resolved by your walking out of the room this morning? (A slow shaking of the head.) The kids thought you were acting strangely, it began your day with a huge negative feeling, and you're ending the day with an extra forty-five minutes in school instead of joining your friends for some fun. Tom, I'm not upset because of what you did to me; I'm upset because of what you did to *you*." He immediately softened, stared, bent his elbow, and rested his head on his open palm. Then, we discussed his reasons for the outburst. Thereafter, I made suggestions as to what he could do the next time he experienced similar feelings.

Following that incident, not only did he smile at me in the corridor for the next two weeks when passing, but also never misbehaved again. Would this tactic work with most twelve-year-old boys? I sincerely doubt it. I'm not suggesting that you throw tennis balls at your back wall to affect a student's behavior. I'm suggesting: Get his attention in a novel way suited solely for him. Take advantage of what you perceive of his personality, and use it to help him. He'll more easily get the message. There was no plan; just a strong hunch from observing the kid. I'd worked my way into his personality and behaved in an unorthodox manner to which he could relate.

Does the unconventional approach I described match your personality? Will it fit most of your students?

If necessary, devise your own creative approach. Remember, however, the important thing is to be different, untraditional, even a bit eccentric— not what they are expecting.

Treating these youngsters in the usual, expected manner will provide positive results with many. However, the teacher who can use unpredictable, unconventional methods with a "difficult" kid or situation stands a much better chance of getting the attention of even more adolescents, as well as nurturing their compliance.

LEARNING FROM EXPERIENCE #5: IT'S *YOUR* RESPONSIBILITY

Butch is talking out of turn again. He's done it three times during this period alone. Time is going by and you need to proceed with the lesson. The only alternative is to remove Butch from class, enabling you to remain on track and complete the lesson…right? *Send him to the principal's office.* There—problem solved!

Nope: Problem is *larger*. Butch will more than likely return to your room on the next day (or in some cases, during the same period following his "talk" with the principal). He is *your* student. He is *your* responsibility. Removing the kid speaks volumes to the class, especially to *him*. Your actions may very well be interpreted as: Mr./Ms. Johnston can't handle Butch…Butch got his way. He received the attention from us that he loves. He got out of working in class…("Everybody watched as *I* interrupted the class.")

You absolutely must take some kind of action, but the plan must already be in existence. The strategy needs to be prepared beforehand. You've no doubt observed the kid in the past; you know what he's capable of doing. Develop your counter-design and have it ready. Why not develop your plan two months before school begins, just in case you need it?

Not sure what to do? Ask a mentor, the guidance counselor…ask a colleague you've observed who appears to be well-seasoned, relaxed, friendly, and willing to help. Call the guy you had as a seventh-grade math teacher who had no difficulty with discipline. Whatever you do, don't simply send him to the office! (Don't forget, whatever you covered with the class while he was gone, you'll have to teach him.)

LEARNING FROM EXPERIENCE #6: THE TEACHER'S ARENA

During my career, I had several student teachers. Here's an incident I recall occurring with one of them; we'll call him Paul. While describing the details of an assignment, Paul sat in the chair behind the teacher's desk and gave the class instructions. During our next discussion, I suggested that, if he truly needed to sit for a short time, he choose a different location. Sit on a table corner, windowsill, student's desk, the sink—anyplace but the "Teacher's Chair."

Do *you* simply sit in the "Teacher's Arena" behind the teacher's desk while addressing your class? I strongly believe that it could easily put you on a different level, at a different frequency—miles away from your students' world. Sitting "behind the desk" limits your ability to maintain the class's attention, appear approachable, exhibit body language and expression, display excitement, maintain control, perceive students' moods, and last but certainly not least, enjoy teaching.

LEARNING FROM EXPERIENCE #7: WATCH YOUR LANGUAGE

No, no, I'm not talking about obscenities. My suggestion is to employ not only classroom-appropriate dialogue, but also words and phrases that work in an optimistic, encouraging manner for your students. Using words and phrases that do not motivate in a positive, sincere fashion (the "wrong language") could imply to them a lack of concern, a sense of disenchantment, dismissiveness, and superiority.

Using the right language projects a sense of interest, sincerity, attentiveness, and respect. This doesn't mean that you need to start collecting a resource of new vocabulary words; it does imply, however, that you prepare a thought process, reminding yourself of your position, your responsibility, and the possibility of your influencing these kids in a positive manner.

Let's look at positive reinforcement. When a student hands in an impressive assignment, or answers a difficult question correctly, you may be tempted to simply reply, "Good job!" Fine, use it *once* per class, even once per month; that's it! To the ears of many adolescents, a response begins to lose sincerity, significance, and power when they hear the same words again and again, especially from the same individual. Consequently, they may not feel as verbally rewarded. The same goes for any other phrases that seem to be shared by far too many parents and educators, such as, "Good answer," "That-a-boy / girl," and so on.

How about an encouraging response that truly gets a pupil's attention and makes the kid feel sincerely, verbally compensated:

- "I am impressed!"

- "I call that progress!"

- "I like the way you handled that?"

- "Thank you, thank you!"

- "Maybe you should be up here, and I should be sitting there."

- "Great, my friend."

- "Super!"

- "Man, are you on the right track!"

- "You make me look good!"

- "I am proud of you."

Be *original*; be sincere. *Yes*, it does make a difference!
And speaking of language usage, read on...

LEARNING FROM EXPERIENCE #8: "OK"

When it's time for the active class discussion to conclude, or the kids must line up at the door in preparation for the field trip, or everyone must give you their attention for anything, what word(s) do you use in obtaining their attention? Is it "OK"—over and over, on every occasion?

Does "OK" become boring, obsolete, and less significant to the kids after they've heard it from the majority of teachers year after year? Does it continually work well in getting a quick response? Want to increase the lack of attention? Just say, "OK!" Can you find another word or words? You can? ...OK!

LEARNING FROM EXPERIENCE #9: CLARITY

Try not to "announce" the beginning of the lesson. You need, of course, to explain the direction of the session, but do not allow your students to get used to a loud declaration, on your part, indicating that you wish them to quiet down. Rather, stand in the middle of the teacher's arena in your "instructor's pose." If necessary, stare at anyone still engaged in conversation. Let them see that, following the bell, you're ready to begin. Do not raise your voice in competition with any noise in the classroom. The interpretation may be that you don't mind a vocal challenge,...that they are permitted to converse until the teacher increases his or her volume. If you allow them to wait for the "shout," they'll more easily assume that they may take the time to complete the conversation prior to listening to the lesson's beginning. Once you have their attention, pause for a few seconds as your eyes sweep back and forth across the room using the "Teacher-stare."

LEARNING FROM EXPERIENCE #10: LESSON PLANS

Are daily lesson plans truly necessary? I recall, on an occasion, hearing a teacher insist that daily lesson plans are, in fact, "a waste of time. I know what I'm doing. I've been doing the same thing for nearly ten years!" exclaimed the individual.

Really?...and the daily progress has been exactly the same with each class for all ten years? Additionally, has the nature of motivation for each group also been the same, along with the guided practice, assignments, organizing skills, attention, and recall? Is this reality?

The instructor needs to consider the ability of each class,...focus upon its progress since the unit was begun and the type of inspirational stimuli required,... not to mention spending quality time creating the perfect strategies to gain the students' attention and interest.

Developing the lesson, absorbing it, modifying it, tweaking it; the plan must be firmly embedded within your brain before you approach the students with it. Are daily lesson plans truly necessary? Absolutely! And what are the tools used to build the lesson?

The labeled tools for lesson construction may differ, depending upon when and where you attended college. Whether or not a teacher employs the terms Anticipatory Set, Introduction, Motivation, Hook, Main Lesson, Development, Procedure, Closure, or Conclusion is not of primary importance. However, a lesson is made up of a beginning, a middle, and an end. And that is what a good teacher needs in formulating a successful experience for a class of young people. This is not to say, however, that each period requires a full "plan-sheet" displaying paragraphs of information. Short phrases and simple "reminding words" in a plan book displaying a full week's program of lessons, notes, and activities are fine. If the lesson constructed developed into a larger intricate plan, I would write down any short necessary components to keep in hand, on my desk, or on a podium for reference.

Would you like to hold on to your plan book so as to possibly include some of the same components next year? Absolutely!...however, we'll assume that modifications may very well be necessary.

When the teacher develops lesson plans, he or she:

- Is able to rely upon the organization of a written set of prepared strategies.

- Has the option of reviewing the lesson's motivation, progress, homework assigned, modifications, etc.

- Has a more precise idea as to the ultimate goal.

- Can view and anticipate the progress through the lesson in a logical order.

- Can view every step of the instructional timeline in a clear and easy manner, and thus better prepare for the teaching process in advance. This visualization increases teacher success potential.

- Can plan more effectively and avoid frustration.

- Has the option to modify or improve the lesson's design.

- Is better able to achieve objectives.

- Has a record of the lesson's progress and components if absent.

- Is able to go back and analyze one's own teaching (what went well, what didn't); then improve on it for its next use.

- May anticipate the students' questions by reviewing the content.

And remember, be flexible. The lesson plan is not a set of directions guiding one in installing an oil filter. Things happen. Be prepared.

LEARNING FROM EXPERIENCE #11: THE NEW KID

There's a knock at your classroom door. It's the guidance counselor, or the principal, or some guy in suit and tie with a smile on his face. Doesn't matter. What *is* important is the fourteen-year-old standing next to him. Yeah, you've already figured it out.

"Good morning, Ms. Farrell, this is Bill Antuda from Nebraska; his family just arrived and he is entering our school system today. He is an eighth-grader, and I've placed him in your class." *A new student*. Oh, no! It's March. How will you possibly catch him up with the work, especially considering that the curriculum in Nebraska is certainly not the same as in your state?

Yes, it will be your responsibility, and it won't be easy. Let's see…now, how can you make this event even more difficult?

- Don't smile at the kid. Just stare at him.

- Ask, "Doesn't Mr. Frank have fewer students in *his* class?"

- "How do I deal with this, sir? It's so late in the year?"

Appear to take a long difficult breath and let your cheeks puff up as you exhale. Then, after pursing your lips, utter, "OK," and return to your room with your new student behind you. Tell him to sit anywhere, leaving the *decision* up to him as to where to insert himself. (Hasn't he got enough to deal with?)

Any of the above responses will no doubt bring about his very best academic effort, right? Sorry, I'm being sarcastic, and I should behave. OK, OK, I'll stop.

How about this:

Extend your hand to him and say, "Hey, Bill, welcome to Disney World. I'll be happy to find you a seat in my room, though I didn't know you were coming and the kids have eaten all the bagels and cream cheese. Nothing left, buddy.

"OK, sometimes I get a bit silly and carried away when I'm hungry."

I know, I know—I do behave rather peculiarly at times. Simply do what you can in your own way to extend an element of friendly comfort. Watch his reaction. Not what he was expecting...good. Can he deal with your wit? If necessary, adjust it. "Welcome to our school, Bill. Nice to meet you. First days can be a bit uncomfortable; however, I think you'll grow to like it here. We've got some great kids. Come, follow me, Bill.

"Class, this is Bill Antuda. He'll be joining us for the remainder of the year. Bill, have a seat right here. (Seat him quickly) Joanne, please inform Bill as to what topic we're studying." Dialogue between Bill and a class member ensues while you briefly get involved in "something" at your desk (allow the "barrier" to be broken). Then, at your first opportunity, corral a trusted student to accompany (lead) the boy to his next class. Between bells, find him. How's he doing?

Interview the kid later; talk to his parents, get his records from the office, or from Nebraska. Reach out to other professionals for help. There *is* an answer to dealing with the curriculum problem; find it!

LEARNING FROM EXPERIENCE #12: KEEP TALKING WHILE SHE'S INTERRUPTING

You have the group's attention; things are going well as you progress toward the conclusion to the lesson. All eyes are upon you...all eyes except Lori's, that is. She's speaking in a whisper again to Betsy. If you stop, however, to scold or ask for her attention, you suffer a disruption. What can you do to deter her behavior?

My advice: Continue teaching and talking while moving toward her desk. With you standing behind her, she's unlikely to continue the conversation. (If her ears turn red, she is totally aware of your presence and has definitely concluded the conversation) Want to be somewhat creative in totally capturing her attention, bringing her back into the fold? After fifteen seconds, direct your words toward a question she can easily answer and call upon her. Try another step? Continue teaching, finding a reason within the next minute or so to refer to her earlier contribution; be certain to mention her name, look at her, and point to her. (The second and third steps may not be totally necessary. However, they usually do work well in bringing Lori back into the lesson's direction.) Then continue moving about the room while teaching. When a student appears to lose interest or begins to bother another, walk toward the kid and simply continue.

LEARNING FROM EXPERIENCE #13: SUCCEED IN YOUR WARNINGS OF ENDANGERMENT

Members of our younger generation are frequently told by adults not to participate in certain perilous behaviors. (Example: "Just say, 'no.'") This approach frequently does not succeed. It is too simple, too easy for them to refuse. Time must be spent with the students involved in an honest discussion and study of the perilous activity. They must be educated in such a way that *they*, themselves, come to totally recognize and understand the existing dangers involved in the risky behaviors. *They* must see the high risk, understand it, and willingly repudiate its engagement.

Most youngsters remain optimistic in relation to events taking place in their lives...and that's O.K. – usually.... There are, however, certain appealing activities that pose a steady, genuine danger to their well-being—smoking, substance abuse, becoming sexually active at an early age, violence, unhealthy diet, and so on.

Now, their optimism gives many eager adolescents an active, positive attitude toward life. Though this may afford them an enjoyable existence much of the time, it may also diminish their perception of danger, reduce common sense, and promote denial. It then, becomes the responsibility of the older generation to clarify and intensify their ability to recognize the existence these threats.

The teacher, however, cannot simply blurt out, "Don't do it!" In order to convince this younger age group, students need to be moved *unconventionally, respectfully, educationally, emotionally, and slowly...in steps, rising level by level, and beginning at a point parallel to their present position and mind-set.* (Need to read that again? So did I.)

THE APPROACH:

The following suggested method can be used in regard to many perilous behaviors. For the purpose of offering an example, I chose the dangers of smoking. Though you may not be a health teacher, this approach can still offer you a realistic look at the adolescent mind and ways to successfully deal with it.

I would instruct my health education class, "Jot down on a piece of paper the main reason why you believe some young people begin smoking." (For decades, the top response in my health classes was, "It's cool," or "It looks cool.")

Follow this piece with the question, "How many of you honestly think that it does look cool?" (*Begin at a point parallel to their present position and mind-set.*)

Respond by accepting their reasoning...to them, it *does* look cool, (or whatever the top response happens to be). Write it down on a board in front of the room. In doing so, you are not agreeing with them; you are declaring that you understand their reasoning and allowing them to have a voice, even if the reasoning is unrealistic. Consequently, you are placing yourself in a friendlier, accepting position: "I understand why you feel this way."

Next question:

"Why are so many adults in opposition to teenage smoking?"

In this segment, their responses will likely offer health dangers which they've frequently heard but, quite possibly, not seriously considered as likely to affect *them*. Let them discuss these responses.

Now it is time to leave the room—not physically, just mentally and educationally.

The next step could be to view the very best informative and relevant video that you can find. It should realistically and sensibly explain why the decision to begin inhaling cigarette smoke is incredibly perilous and sense-less. This could be a video that realistically displays actual views of affected human lungs, destroyed cilia, cancer tumors, hospital patients with gravelly voices, etc.…. The individuals in the presentation need to be authentic, med-ical professionals or individuals physically affected by smoke inhalations, not actors. Use significant information and irrefutable proof.

More discussion should follow the video, with no lecturing by the teacher. Allow class members to offer comments based upon the video's information.

"Does anyone in the room know someone that has suffered in similar ways? It is not necessary to mention names." Keep the discussion going. "Does that person still smoke? Did she attempt to quit? Why do you think she didn't succeed?"

In the next class session, perhaps offer transparencies, photographs, quotes from doctors, or any kind of overwhelming documented evidence. Let these be fodder for more discussion.

Following that, it is time for first-hand testimonies from those affected by cigarette smoking…former smokers, witnesses, nurses, retired doctors, radiologists, X-ray technicians, a letter / e-mail / or phone call from the Mayo Clinic, National Institute of Health, county health center, Centers for

Disease Control, etc. Invite one or two nearby professionals to your classroom to offer a presentation. Class members will have been inundated with indisputable, clear evidence. The majority will find it very difficult to refute the "no-smoking message." Let more discussion follow these presentations.

Next, introduce factual information not yet discussed.

"The Centers for Disease Control recently announced that the average smoker loses eleven years of life because of smoking. However, that's only an average. I'm sure that some smokers lose only four or five years of living rather than eleven." Pause for clarity…four or five *years*. "Four or five years, four or five birthdays, four or five Christmases…." Pause….

"Then again, if eleven is the *average*, I suppose some lose nineteen or twenty years of life." Write them on a board in front of the room. Large numbers. "19–20."

Move to another part of the board and, in order to truly underscore the serious reality of your message, begin writing the months of the year. When you reach June, quietly enlist the help of several students to join you by creating their own list of months visible to all. Let it go on for a while, until nine, eleven, or even nineteen yearly lists of months are displayed. Take the time; have the class join together in reading the months aloud.

Long pause. Discussion.

This will take several days, of course. However, by the time you reach this stage in your lessons, their judgment may very well have moved more closely parallel to your point of view.

Regardless of the topic,…smoking, prejudice, healthy diet, bonding, substance abuse, violent behavior, human sexuality, discipline, public speaking,…. (Worth repeating)…the teacher stands a much stronger chance of succeeding if he/she moves unconventionally, respectfully, educationally, emotionally, slowly,…in steps, rising level by level, beginning at a point parallel to the students' present position and mind-set.

Following this type of step-by-step, non-lecturing method, your students have, I believe, a better chance of selecting a wiser direction in making life choices. They are not *instructed* as to what to do; they are encouraged to respectfully make *their own decisions* after overwhelming, persuasive evidence is introduced to them in a unintimidating manner. Sufficient time is given for thought and discussion. Evidence is offered thoroughly and clearly from excellent sources. They are treated respectfully, sincerely, as though you care—and, of course, you do. Encourage honest responses during a discussion. After several class members voluntarily share their decisions not to smoke (and this will occur), it is time for *your* clear and honest opinion stated slowly, dramatically, and sensibly explaining perhaps, how and when you made the same decision as they. The more emotional the revelation, the greater its effect, and the more easily they may come to identify with it.

LEARNING FROM EXPERIENCE #14: THE TEACHERS' CONFERENCE

You've attended a conference with several colleagues. There were a number of speakers and the majority of the information was rather new, unique, and considered useful. As the day continued, you compared your notes with your colleagues' and, during lunch, jotted down some helpful material that you missed. On the way home, the group of you discussed the enlightening knowledge and agreed that the experience was worth the trip. Is that it? The experience is completed?

No. Now you must spend energy within a very brief time span planning how to utilize the new skills and information. Do not "put it on hold!" You've heard the expression, "Use it or lose it?" The longer you wait, the less likely you will be to introduce it to your classes. Review the information with your colleagues. Perhaps discuss with them your classes' responses to the material's introduction. Keep the dialogue ongoing. You say you already knew this? Fine, simply treat this message as a reminder.

LEARNING FROM EXPERIENCE #15: TOUCHING

Some of them move right in: one hand on the top of your desk and the other hand on your shoulder. They need it? They like it? They're used to it?

Does touching give them a feeling of bonding, affection, attention? If it is an appropriate kind of touching, and you still have the individual's educational attention, why can't it continue? Are you all right with it? I had to adjust to it,…wasn't ready,…didn't know it would occur. Then, following my introduction to it, adjustment to it, and understanding of it, I applied it. I touched them! In fun, in support, in making better contact, in allowing them to know that I liked them and *cared*.

Keep in mind… the ones that often give the impression that they don't wish to be touched, are the ones that frequently need it and may ultimately respond to it in a positive manner.

LEARNING FROM EXPERIENCE #16: BECOMING HUMAN

Arrange one or two family photos on your desk. When students see them, it may be easier for them to picture you in a lifestyle familiar to them. "My teacher is married!" "My teacher is a mom/a dad." Rather than being seen as the person who enters a classroom environment distributing papers, assignments, directions, and commands, you begin to come across as being more human—more like a mom or dad, or even more like themselves—human!

After they've seen your family photos, you may find them staring at you for periods of time. Good! Could be a sign of understanding, acceptance, or even fondness.

SECTION THREE:

TOOLS THAT SUCCEED: UNCONVENTIONAL APPROACHES AND STRATEGIES

CHAPTER 6: UNIQUE AND UNORTHODOX APPROACHES IN EDUCATION

From time to time, you'll notice my use of the term, "unorthodox." My own definition of the word would be unconventional, untraditional, thought-provoking, unexpected, or inspiring. Using common, expected, conventional methods in one's teaching can succeed with many students. But these methods are not likely to *always* produce substantial curiosity, attention, or progress with *all* students. In the following chapter, I present several approaches I categorize as different or unorthodox. I believe you'll find them useful. Numerous other unconventional activities can be found in chapters 8 and 9. My students found them thought-provoking, motivating, even fascinating. Try something different—something that they'll find inspiring.

———

Weird Teacher: The following scene, or one quite similar, has repeated itself more than once over my years in the classroom:

Students (and teacher) busily working in silence....

I glance up briefly to check on their progress. A student is sitting, staring at me. I whisper, "What?"

She responds (with no smile whatsoever), "Mr. Sgambato, you're weird."

"Thank you," I quickly reply. And then, shortly following, "Do you mean weird-good or weird-bad?"

After a short pause, "Weird-good...I guess."

"Would you rather that I was more of an un-weird teacher so you'd know exactly what to expect in each of my daily lessons?"

Very quickly, "No, no, no." Then, finally a smile.

Apparently, some students, when finished with a particular task, stared around the room with mind searching for thought. That's when they would spot me, and were reminded of my "weirdness."

Please consider my translation of the above exchange:

- "Weird" = unorthodox approach to kids and to education.

- "Would you rather that I was more of an un-weird teacher so you'd know exactly what to expect in each of my daily lessons?" "No, no, no." = Continue dealing with students in the same manner; it gives them a feeling of interest, freedom, friendship, eccentricity, and enjoyment.

My "weirdness" may be, in part, attributed to my personality, but my unorthodox methods would not have blossomed so fully had it not been for a number of unique education courses and people, foremost of which were Jerry Edwards and Phil Olynciw, representatives of Project Team. Unconventional activities, when engaged by most educators, serve to help in attaining student involvement, attention, amusement, and appreciation. Try it. (More about Jerry and Phil later.)

Treat them like kids. That is, approach them from *their* direction, getting their complete attention in an unorthodox manner that would truly be motivating to *them*. Think as they do.

An unconventional tactic quickly gathers their attention, inspires their thought processes, and gets your point across in the most potentially successful manner. Being different may also persuade these young people to take a closer look at their teacher...and thusly, you may come off as unusual, cool, strange, or even "weird," but worthy of watching and a teacher, perhaps, to whom they listen. They can easily tell when the teacher sees the world through their eyes, understands them and accepts them for who they are. Your classroom can be unique, atypical. Your students can, thusly, be drawn into your lesson by instinct and interest. What could be better?

An excellent time for irregular, quirky dialogue is on the first day of school.

THE FIRST DAY OF SCHOOL

I miss the first day of school enormously; the presence of twenty-some ten and eleven-year-olds offering a collection of facial expressions and moods—looks of anticipation, fatigue, confusion, skepticism, joy, and uncertainty.

Early in the period, they expect to hear teacher-type phrases like, "Sit wherever you like"..."Please copy the list of materials from the board while waiting." Go ahead and deliver such comments. When all are settled, however, it is time for the teacher to offer the unexpected, unconventional comments; short sentences that will catch their attention, hold their eyes, appeal to their imagination, make them think, wonder, and look forward to the next day. Here's one that I used numerous times in my English class:

"I've got some disappointing news for you." With lips pursed, I would pause and move my eyes around the room, being certain that I had their attention. "There will be no book reports accepted from anyone this year in my English class. I'm sorry, but that's the way it is." They, of course, would appear somewhat stunned and a bit confused. Every reading teacher they'd experienced up to that point, certainly, had employed "The Book Report." They would silently look around at classmates as they attempted to clarify the message and deal with their surprisingly good fortune. Then gradually, they'd turn again to me. Subsequently, perhaps, a few smiles and tiny squeals of joy would emerge. Following the peculiar announcement, I would describe my actual approach to reading, which I felt was unique, more enjoyable, and far more effective than traditional methods. You may wish to do something similar, and then divulge your real plan—truly different, really cool, and approached, perhaps, in an unconventional manner.

The imaginative announcement that you divulge about your course will naturally be of your choosing. Just be unorthodox. Additionally, why not confront the obvious? On that first day of school, follow up with something like, "It's tough giving up summer. I can still remember leaving my home on my first day of school, saying good-bye to my dog and heading up the road carrying all my school supplies while thinking, 'I hope today goes OK' Did anyone have any particular feelings, today?" There may be interest in pursuing the topic, "The First Day of School," for a bit. If that's the case, fine. Encourage responses. Get them talking. Be careful not to be critical of what you hear. Capture their attention, and gently "reel them in." They will begin to relax a bit during the discussion; they'll also <u>begin to know the teacher better</u>.

Then, after a bit of time, while engaging all the eyes in the room, perhaps offer something like, "I think you're going to like it here. I can't wait to get started. I will do my best to present an interesting course and not bore you. So, uh...please try not to bore *me*." Allow them the opportunity to get used to your voice, your manner, your enthusiasm for teaching. The instructor must assure them that they are safe, among friends, and that things will be fine. However, they *will* be challenged. During the dialogue, walk the room; don't simply occupy the "teacher's arena" delivering first-day information. Move closer; allow heads to turn. Encourage it. Get closer to them. Read their eyes; let them read yours. Offer a sincere, receptive expression, and maintain your very best attention. If you're able to retain their eye contact, the students will usually experience difficulty hiding the truth from you. You can, then, summon your perceptive ability and have it go to work for you. Who are they, really? What's going on in their minds? Get to know your students.

The rest of the time will be taken up, of course, with fire drill instructions, classroom rules and expectations, a discussion of materials, scheduling questions, etc.. On the next day of school, begin developing a positive classroom atmosphere by taking the first step in creating a *Team* of students. Help them in acquiring better cooperative and team-building skills, along with building trust, and developing the courage to stand out and take positive risks—a willingness to *try*. (Suggestions as to how to go about developing the Team approach begin with chapter 7. Please look it over)

It isn't likely that any group of students, on its own, could focus, work as a team, and effectively promote bonding and cooperation. My yearly plan was to address this educational necessity at my first opportunity. Additionally, I've always felt a strong need to subtly assure the kids that my classroom could possibly be considerably different from the majority of experiences they'd already had.

"IT ISN'T FAIR"

You've heard the words, "It's not fair!" or, "School's not fair!" Some teachers may be tempted to respond, "Well, life's not fair…"

Really? Life isn't fair to us? Might the adolescent thereafter entertain the notion, "What did I do to deserve an unfair life?" Or, "Then why try?" Think about it; is the response at all helpful?

How about addressing the cause of the outburst or encouraging a short discussion, instead of just whisking away the student's emotional complaint with an impractical statement?

Or, consider an additional possibility:

Following the complaint(s), suggest a discussion (taking place immediately or planned for a later time) based on what some see as the unfairness of school. When the opportunity for discussion arrives, engage the topic by asking everyone to respond to a request:

"Write down two things that are unfair about school." Allow sufficient time.

Explain that difficulties within the school environment are like all difficulties; the individual experiencing the problem is not always able to perceive a quick solution, but help is available. Then, pair off into groups of two for a conversation based upon ways school is perceived as unfair.

Allow each student to voice a complaint concerning the unfairness of school. Then, offer the partners an opportunity to help. What can be done about the complaints? Explain that you'd like to give each student an opportunity to suggest a remedy in helping the classmate deal with what is seen as difficult or "unfair." The technique used in this lesson is to write "prescriptions" for the difficulties. Generally speaking, "prescriptions" are what doctors give patients to make them *feel better*. Likewise, this activity gives everyone an opportunity to recommend a "remedy" for a variety of different concerns in order to help a classmate "*feel better*." We must keep in mind that some complaints will not be resolved by a conversation with one other individual. Therefore, this activity can be followed by repeating it in groups of four or an open class discussion.

When the complaints are shared with the entire class, students can think about "prescriptions" and write them down on paper. One option might be to have the proposed solutions remain anonymous. The approach on the part of a student offering a prescription could begin: "For those of you not having enough time to visit lockers between classes, I suggest the following:..."

All "prescriptions" could be placed in a container and read aloud by individuals over the course of a day or two (devoting short periods of time) for all to hear, or they could be delivered directly to the individual in need. If anyone wishes to report back to the class on engaging the "remedy," this would be an appropriate possibility.[2]

When my students complained that school wasn't fair, I paused for a moment, then responded honestly, "I think you're right. You walk into a classroom, sit in a hard chair, and can't get up to walk around. You have to listen to some man or woman talk about what he or she thinks is important for forty-three minutes. You then have three minutes to get to another room, where it starts all over again.

"You are sometimes forced to study a subject that doesn't appeal to you and have to take work home when you leave the school…. Yeah, I agree, in a strong way, it just doesn't sound fair.

"But, you know what? Presently, **it's the best we have to offer!** I would love to be able to change some things to make the whole day more appealing. By gosh, I'd get bean bags for everybody, change the fluorescent lights to softer illumination, add wall-to-wall carpeting in every classroom, put in a swimming pool and an outdoor ropes course. Then, I'd arrange a hike or dance every month. Yeah, that's what I'd do. I, however, don't have the authority, so here's what *I* say...

"Do whatever the heck you need to do to make it through. Tell your younger brother not to come into your bedroom when you're doing your homework, go for your own hikes on weekends with pals, treat yourself to the best novels and movies you can find, get plenty of sleep, tell terrific jokes to your friends, laugh until you fall on the floor, cry when you're sad, volunteer at a dog kennel and maybe take home a black lab. Just do it...whatever you have to do...put in six years of your best work! *Do It!* (Delivered with considerable volume.)

After a pause, with a softer tone: "Then, not that long from now, when your name is called, walk across the stage wearing your cap and gown and accept your diploma. Following that, go to as many graduation parties as you can. Then *leave town!* When you're eighteen or nineteen, leaving town won't seem quite as intimidating as it may appear right now. Further your education; pursue your dream. In time, maybe even get married after a few years. Want to move back here? Terrific, I'll be glad to see you. Bring your degree with you. You'll be making more money than I, but that's OK; I'll still like you.....***Just do it!!*** " (Oh, yeah—you do have to raise your voice a bit to really capture their attention; it drives it home more strongly and shows them how intensely you believe in it.)

This might also be a good time to pursue a second step to the experience: "Write down two things that you *like* about school." Take the same approach you did earlier.

Perhaps some kids are overlooking some of the pleasant, more positive things about the school setting. If they think about it, they will come up with a list. And, if no one mentions how important these kids are to their teachers and school personnel who work with them, remind them—enthusiastically!

One of the complaints vocalized during the last activity was, more than likely, something about homework. The following approach was unquestionably helpful to my colleagues and myself.

RECIPE FOR HOMEWORK SUCCESS

(The following activity includes all lesson details used in its development. I suggest initially reading it in its entirety. If the reader, at a later time, wishes to engage the shorter, formatted "lesson plan" version, it exists within the appendix – <u>Lesson #1</u>)

Because concerns and complaints about homework are frequently exchanged among class members, the following task might help the class find productive solutions to their problems.

- Initiate a discussion about homework, allowing your pupils to talk about the daily responsibilities in any manner they wish—even venting. Then, divide students into groups of two, directing them to focus upon complaints expressed by classmates earlier in the lesson and discuss ways of addressing the concerns in a positive fashion. (Each student may take brief notes.)

- After bringing the group back together in a total class Community Meeting (described later), ask that they brainstorm solutions to one concern at a time as you write them clearly on Smartboard, newsprint, etc.

Following that, propose that the suggestions be included in a "Recipe for Homework Success," (a list of strategies to be considered by classmates). How can they help each other succeed?

Each item may be written on the board, newsprint, or screen at the front of the room and discussed thoroughly. When the class is satisfied with the coverage and the possible benefit of the suggestions, print them clearly and neatly. Display the list. Additionally, copy the information on individual sheets to be passed out among the kids.

The following is a list of those suggestions mentioned most often in my classes:

1. Don't forget to use your assignment pad or iPad, etc. for recording homework assignments.

2. Be sure that you understand the directions before leaving school.

3. Make good use of study halls.

4. Organize your materials in your binder and in your locker.

5. Do your work at the same time daily, <u>early</u>; follow a schedule.

6. Find a quiet, comfortable place to work, away from the TV.

7. Don't procrastinate.

8. Take a break if you have a lot to do.

9. Put completed homework in a place where you won't lose or forget it.[3]

Perhaps conclude by asking class members to write down ways in which they may benefit through the use of the suggestions on the list. In class, refer to the list as necessary, or add to it.

Kindly keep my earlier description of Robert in mind (the boy whose home I visited).

Homework assumes that there *is* a "Home."

———

EARLYBIRD SPECIAL:

My former colleague, Tom Murray, initiated the use of the "Earlybird Special," a useful strategy in persuading students to be time-conscious. On days when he planned to give a pop quiz (a "shotgun"), he placed a bonus question on the board right beneath the room's map. At precisely 30 seconds before the tardy bell rang, the map was pulled down to conceal the bonus question. Anyone arriving after that time missed the opportunity to obtain the bonus points. This encouraged students to get to class as early as possible on a regular basis, especially since they did not know, in advance, when there would be a "shotgun."

LET'S DO IT DIFFERENTLY

An example of what you can do when sensing a "better way" of undertaking a goal.

I pledge allegiance to the Flag of the United States of America, and to the Republic... During your career, there may be moments when you see a better way to do something. It may be an element of the curriculum or a part of the daily routine. You may suddenly visualize a superior procedure, a more positive outcome, a better, realistic approach,...simply, a potentially more successful method of getting something done. What should you do?

For several months, all classrooms in our building had participated in reciting the Pledge of Allegiance by following a student leading them over the public address system. With hand over my heart, I watched the eyes of my sixth-grade students as they stood next to their desks, verbally working their way through each word, each line.....

The entire class mouthed the familiar words day after day, week after week. Their eyes, however, revealed the truth: my kids were not listening to the significance of the language, the meaning...the message meant little to them because of the manner in which the Pledge had been approached. It simply became part of the morning ritual, like taking attendance, listening to morning announcements, getting pen and binders ready. While they recited, heads turned, lips smiled, eyes rolled. All continued to quietly recite, yet their minds were elsewhere. Their mouths were operating "on automatic." My thought: What if the Pledge of Allegiance remains dull, empty, and meaningless in the minds of these eleven- and twelve-year-olds? This state of affairs had to end immediately.

It was the student council organization that was responsible for the activity. I didn't want to offend the young teacher in charge or cause any problem for the organization. So, the next morning, I simply announced to my class that we would no longer participate in the morning pledge. The looks were confused. Eyes lowered,...silence filled the room. I gave them several days for the confusion and questions to escalate in their minds. Every single morning, we sat quietly as the rest of the school recited the Pledge of Allegiance along with the public address system.

On the afternoon of the third day, I took a bright, active student aside and described to him how I felt the Pledge of Allegiance *should* be recited—with clarity and sensitivity. "We should say each word firmly, slowly, pronounced absolutely correctly, with real <u>meaning</u>...and not take our eyes off the flag...kids should feel encouraged to <u>think</u> about the words." We talked about my reasoning for a few minutes.

I then asked if he would lead the class in the pledge on the following day, also requesting him to avoid disclosing our conversation and our "plan." (By the way, I chose the right kid.)

On the following morning, on cue, he stood and announced that he wanted to recite the Pledge of Allegiance. I asked if he wished to recite it alone. He replied, "Yes," (just as planned). The recitation went just as I'd asked, slowly, loudly, and with abundant feeling.

He was great! There were whispers of, "Wow!"..."I can't believe it."... "Is he going to do that every morning?"

I then asked him to repeat the words; this time, one line at a time. As he finished each line, I asked for an interpretation from the class. "What exactly does 'indivisible' mean?" They were motivated, interested, and enthusiastic. It was *different*. Attention was totally focused on word meaning and significance. We ran out of time and had to continue the next morning.

We never re-joined the rest of the school in droning the pledge along with the PA. Instead, once a week, a different student volunteered to rehearse and lead our class in the same slow, deliberate and meaningful way. That was how my classes recited the Pledge of Allegiance for the next few years. Fortunately, I was never approached by administration, teacher, or parent with concerns or questions. (Hard to believe)

Several times, when unexpectedly meeting former students, I was reminded of the unorthodox approaches I used as their teacher...this was one of them occasionally mentioned. Eventually, the building's recital of the pledge was dropped from the school's morning events, (but not from mine).

When it suddenly occurs to you, "There is a better way of doing this," what can you do?....

What will *you* do?

CHAPTER 7: ARE YOU LISTENING?

Do you enjoy teaching? You do! Great! It would follow, I believe, that you enjoy kids. That is fortunate...because occasions will more than likely occur where you'll find yourself placed in a position of impending responsibility as you're approached by a student in need...in need of what? In need of *you*! This is the kid who is looking for understanding, advice, attention, possibly even safety—and most importantly, someone to *listen* to her. And somewhere along the line, she got the notion that you could supply what is missing in her life at that particular time. For those of you with years of experience...this has more than likely already occurred. Individuals new to the profession...prepare for this; it **will** more than likely occur.

Included in this chapter are some responses and techniques I believe you could employ on those occasions when you're driving into the parking lot a bit early, sitting at your desk at 3:45 correcting papers, or saying goodnight to the school secretary,...and are approached by a student in need. (easily perceived; it's in the facial expression,... especially, of course, the eyes).

First of all, when it becomes obvious that she wishes to talk to you, be certain that enough time is available. If not, briefly explain to her that you are absolutely interested in carrying on the conversation. However for her benefit, you need an occasion where you'll not be required to deal with interruptions as well as having enough time and space to be at your best. So...if necessary, arrange an appointment. Stress the importance of the meeting and how <u>strongly</u> you wish to engage in the discussion.

Then, when the time is right, please consider keeping responses in mind similar to those below:

- Make solid eye contact and lean into the conversation.

- Be accepting, even if you initially disagree with something she says.

- As she is speaking, use "cultural fillers" ("Is that right?" "I understand." "Really!" "Uh-huh.") In this way, the speaker knows you are listening intently.

- Encourage more communication: "Tell me more." "Would you like to talk about it?" "How did you feel about that?" "Then, what happened?"

Use Reflective Listening: Feed back to the speaker words that disclose how you perceive her; listen to the feelings behind the speaker's remarks.

Sometimes, *you* end up informing the *youngster* how she feels. "Sounds like he made you pretty angry." "You seem really sad." "You sound anxious about this concern." "I'll bet that's very frustrating to you." "You really get angry when he says that, don't you."

The most <u>powerful</u> inquiry (when offered at precisely the right time): After you notice a student's facial expression move toward an even darker sadness, or when a break occurs in her voice, or possibly a long pause, you then can ask the most influential question: (slowly and softly) *"How are you feeling right now?"* Pause....

What is the number one response from a kid who has reached this point in relating a sorrowful experience? Yes, you're right...tears. I believe that there's nothing wrong with this. You know what they say about a "good cry." When it's time to cry, we should cry; when it's time to laugh, we laugh. Laughing and crying balance our emotions, our lives. Additionally, it may prompt the student to offer even more information about the event than she prepared to, or in some cases, was even <u>aware of</u>. Be patient and place a supportive hand on her shoulder.

Paraphrase: Let the speaker know that you've heard her by repeating it in your own words:

"So, you're feeling quite lonely right now because she told you she would call to discuss the dance coming up this weekend and didn't. Am I correct?"

Summarize: Highlight the main points.

"Here's what I hear you saying…"

"If I understand you correctly, you're saying that…" Condense it.

Barriers to communication may occur when the teacher is responding only to the facts rather than the speaker's feelings.

- Do not offer quick solutions. "Quick-fix" remedies may give the student the impression that you think she is "not smart enough" to figure it out alone.

- Avoid making quick judgments: "You're taking this too seriously." "I'd just stop talking to that person if I were you." This does not help.

- Do not minimize the problem: "I'm sure you'll feel differently about this in a week or so." Again, it is not the solution to the existing problem for the kid.

- Don't take the floor away from the speaker by interjecting your experience concerning a similar problem: "The same thing happened to me; here's what I did."[4]

During this conversation, you are justifying his feelings, his reaction to the event, and even any confusion he is possibly experiencing. Additionally, remember, you are providing his number one need – someone who will listen intently and remain silent. That's right; the number one need…someone who will listen, just listen.

Be prepared; you may find time flying by, but think of what you are do-ing for this kid. This may be exactly what is needed. Will she feel better? More than likely. Will she remember? What do you think? And what about her self-confidence? Yes, frequently stronger. You were there for her; that means a great deal to these kids.

Now, I'm not suggesting that you can do the same kind of work that a clinical psychologist does. You must be careful in knowing when to suggest a visit to the school psychologist or guidance counselor. However, if the student approaches you, what else should you do at that particular time other than be of help....

Some educators may not see it as part of their job. They may wish to accept no part of the responsibility. If this is their desire, then so be it. In that case, perhaps a referral can promptly be made to another qualified professional.

CHAPTER 8: COOPERATIVE ENVIRONMENT

Here are a few team-building activities that can promote communication and positive attitudes among your students, enabling them to work together more effectively within a cooperative environment.

TEAMBUILDING ACTIVITIES

Activity #1: The Milling Assassin
Activity #2: Encouraging Positive Communication
Activity #3: Developing the Classroom Contract
Activity #4: Seat of Distinction (included as <ins>Chapter 9</ins>)

Activities #1, #2, and #3, above, were created by Dr. Gerald Edwards, Phil Olynciw, and their colleagues, associated with the Northeast Regional Center for Drug-Free Schools and Communities. Dr. Edwards was chairman of the Health Education Department of Adelphi University in Garden City, New York, and director of the Adelphi University National Training Institute, sponsored by the United States Office of Education. I, along with a number of other teachers, experienced a powerfully stimulating ten-day workshop (Project Team) created by this knowledgeable and inspirational group of professionals. The program was sponsored by NYS Division of Substance Abuse Services. Gerry and Phil are the two educators who most strongly influenced my creative abilities and inspired my attitude toward education. I'm certain they have had similar influence upon hundreds of others.

Before moving directly into the **Teambuilding Activities**, I would like to introduce you to one of Gerry and Phil's exceedingly successful creations. The **Community Meeting** is extremely helpful, not only as the environment for the activities contained in this chapter, but within any lesson designed to have students totally absorb a topic while feeling connected, supported, and actively involved. This class session designed and promoted by these men works smoothly, effectively, and is one of the most time-efficient activities I used in my career.

The Community Meeting: A setting within which students are free to pursue a relevant topic, asking and answering questions along with stating opinions relating to the issue. Consequently, they can review, debate, and progress with a better understanding of the subject in a timely fashion. This activity increases better community interaction and helps to build a positive support system among participants. As opinions are generated, the teacher may record the views in the front of the room for all to see. One of the rules is, "No raising of hands." Once the format is understood, experienced, and accepted, students work effectively and efficiently within the environment.

RATIONALE:

The lesson provides-

- Feedback from students on a recently learned subject or a relevant topic being discussed.

- A forum within which to answer questions, offer opinions, and clarify information based upon a particular subject.

Allows for

- Reinforcement of learning.

- Building support and confidence among participants.

- A sharing of positive and negative feelings.

- A large amount of interaction among participants.

- Exploration of further issues.

Rules:

- Stay on task; keep to the "here and now."

- Only one person speaks at a time.

- No hand-raising.

- Share thoughts with the entire group, not the individual sitting next to you.

- When speaking, use the pronoun, "I," speaking only for yourself, rather than collectively ("we").

Jerry Edwards and Phil Olynciw called the next two activities—The Milling Assassin and Developing the Classroom Contract—"humanizing" sessions. The approaches each help develop an atmosphere of friendly exchange. The instructor needs students to participate, cooperate, and work as a team. The following activities help create just that...an environment of positive relationships that serve to enhance teamwork and then learning. I will describe three of the *humanizing* sessions in the following paragraphs, and one of my own in chapter 9.

ACTIVITY #1: THE MILLING ASSASSIN

(The following activity includes all lesson details used in its development. I suggest initially reading it in its entirety. If the reader, at a later time, wishes to engage the shorter, formatted "lesson plan" version, it exists within the appendix – Lesson #2)

The Milling Assassin is an introductory activity I learned at a Project Team workshop. It functions as a "first step" in the process of peer acceptance, bonding, and teambuilding. Though it may sound rather strange at first, it has benefits not immediately perceived. When I first learned of it, I remained uncertain of its potential. Then, I tested it out—with totally positive results. I used it yearly. It works. Try it.

Interacting + bonding = better communication

The Milling Assassin is used as an energizer for the kids, an ice-breaker. It opens the door to the humanizing phenomenon, helping participants see classmates in a different light while encouraging the kids to interact with each other through unique and unconventional techniques. Furthermore, it helps build trust among class members. It is the type of endeavor that they, most likely, never experienced during the first week of school. Participants move about, totally involved, chuckling, even touching. While interacting in this activity, they begin to view their peers (and ultimately their teacher) as who they truly are. If you happen to view any uncomfortable behavior, you may wish to capitalize on it by later discussing why those feelings were understandably experienced. The individuals displaying those particular behaviors remain anonymous.

Introduction: I've presented this activity to groups ranging in age from eleven to adult.

Procedure: The two strategies suggested below are, in my opinion, helpful in "setting the stage"…getting the group in an appropriate frame of mind. However, if you are experiencing time restraints, one or both can be eliminated if necessary.

1. Introduce the following: What are two strategies that help us in dealing with personal problems, discomfort, disappointment? Written on a board in the front pf the room: A <u>Support Network</u> and a <u>Sense of Humor</u>)

   a. **Support network**: Friends and family members available to be approached with personal concerns. "When you are experiencing any kind of difficulties—school problems, personal problems, health concerns, etc.—and feel a need for support and advice, what steps can you take?"
   You can seek trusted friends and family. This is essential for everyone. We all need this type of assistance at times in our lives.

      • Without disclosing names, each student is encouraged to have one or more friends or family members in mind during this part of the lesson.

      • Briefly discuss examples of support experienced by teacher and class members along with the advantages of utilizing the assistance.

   b. **An active sense of humor**: Humor can help "reframe" potentially depressing situations, promote the release of endorphins, and assist in building resilience within an individual. A well-functioning sense of humor helps one see difficult conditions in a different, more realistic manner. One can laugh at a situation more easily and respond to life's struggles more effectively with humor rather than anger.

      • Offer amusing occurrences from your life that helped you deal with challenging times from your past.

      • Ask for humorous examples from the class. Brief discussion. Then, taking advantage of their amused frames of mind, move immediately from the existing humorous environment into the activity described below:

Members of the class stand and form a circle, eyes closed, hands behind their backs. The facilitator moves around the outside of the circle pulling upon the index finger of each participant—all except for the student secretly chosen by the facilitator to portray the Milling Assassin. His or her finger is ignored. Instead, the middle of the palm is touched. (The individual was not forewarned.) With that, the teacher announces, "Go ahead and mill." Kids can be reminded that it is a nonverbal activity (no talking at all). They wander about the front of the room, shaking hands with classmates. If they giggle a bit, that is helpful in breaking the ice, the barriers. Whenever the Assassin feels he or she can get away with it, along with shaking the hand, the index finger is extended to touch the wrist area of the unsuspecting classmate. With that, the individual receiving the "Death Tap" (as the teacher earlier instructed) silently counts to ten, then falls to the floor, making any appropriate vocal noises he or she may wish. No one else may, at that time, say a word about who is suspected as the Assassin. Counting to ten allows the Assassin to move away from the "victim" and not be easily identified.

If a student feels he or she knows who the Assassin is, he or she may raise a hand and ask the facilitator to stop the action. The facilitator then asks the class for a second individual to raise a hand in order to "back up" the guess yet to be made by the first individual. (You need two participants involved to officially offer a guess as to the identity of the Assassin.)

After someone volunteers to "back up" the first student, he or she is then given the opportunity to identify the Assassin. If the individuals are correct, the Assassin has been successfully identified and the first session concludes. If the individuals are incorrect, both also die and fall to the floor.

Continue milling until the "culprit" is identified.

This activity gives students opportunities to see different characteristics of their classmates' personalities. It helps by bringing to the surface personal traits that are not frequently visible within a classroom environment. By discovering other dimensions of their classmates' characters, they get to know one another better as well as become more accepting.

The "ice" has been broken.[5]

"PROCESSING" THE ACTIVITY:

Processing is a procedure that offers a "look back," a manner of reviewing an activity in such a way that the participants better understand its purpose as well as examine what they were thinking and doing during the flow. They may then more easily perceive the benefits of engaging the lesson and what can be learned from it.

Processing could include the use of helpful questions such as:

- "Why do you think I introduced the lesson?"

- "What did you learn?"

- "What surprised you?"

- "What kind of classmate would really enjoy this activity?"

- "What would you change in the activity to make the lesson better?"

- "How are you feeling about what we just did?"

The processing component may include feedback from the teacher describing what he or she had observed (no names need be mentioned). Observations might include the speed with which the activity was initiated, the types of conversations exchanged, how many got out of their chairs first or last, how many approached a classmate quickly, slowly, quietly, enthusiastically, how many smiled, etc.. This approach allows the class an opportunity to understand the participants' different interpretations of the task. It can encourage more enthusiastic behavior on the part of some kids in future lessons, regardless of the type of activities engaged by your students.

Example: "I observed several rise from their chairs rather quickly and begin searching for a classmate with whom to shake hands. The majority of the class, however, rose more slowly, heads turning to look around the room, and did not seem to be in a hurry. This appears rather normal for a group this size. I've seen the same reaction with seventh graders, high school seniors, teachers, and parents. Now I could be wrong, but some seemed…well…a bit reluctant at first, to get moving, but then eventually joined in. Why do you suppose some moved in this fashion?"

During the discussion, a class member may offer something similar to the following: "They were uncertain / hesitant / looked a bit uncomfortable in becoming involved." Participants are then free to conclude that this "uncertainty" is common and normal—and thus, if they hesitated to become immediately involved, they should not be concerned; it's typical. Consequently, with greater confidence during the next activity (whatever that may be), they'll not likely hold back as much.

Perhaps, conclude with, "The truth is—I enjoyed every moment!"

Processing helps everyone understand how the class is doing and validates the reality that some class members have different perceptions and reactions to the task (as well as to life, itself). They might, therefore, come to recognize that their classmates may be viewing the lesson in a different manner. Consequently, this perception may possibly give them a new perspective on the activity as well as on their peers. Additionally, some may respond to future encounters with greater enthusiasm and optimism.

Repeat the activity if is there is time and interest.[6]

If your response to this activity is, "You gotta be kidding!" I do understand, but hold on. As I indicated earlier, I have repeatedly witnessed unorthodox approaches working again and again. Additionally, the Milling Assassin is almost unanimously accepted by participants of all ages. Catch them a bit off guard; employ totally unsuspected types of engagements; show them that your approach is distinctive and applied with them in mind. Unsure? Perhaps, return to the introduction of this section and read again the activity's purpose. Then decide.

ACTIVITY #2: ENCOURAGING POSITIVE COMMUNICATION

A. INTRODUCTION TO SUCCESSFUL LISTENING:

(The following activity includes all lesson details used in its development. I suggest initially reading it in its entirety. If the reader, at a later time, wishes to engage the shorter, formatted "lesson plan" version, it exists within the appendix – <u>Lesson #3a</u>)

At this point, it would be advantageous to revisit a topic I described earlier in chapter 7, titled "Are You Listening?" This was a lesson devoted to skills used in successfully listening to one's students. This time, it's the *kids'* turn to *listen to each other.*

I suggest that you begin with some or all of the following questions on screen, board, or newsprint:

How well do members of our society listen to each other?

- How do you know when an individual is listening to you? (One can judge by behavior, body language, facial expressions, etc.)

- How do you know when an individual is *not* listening to you?

- How does one feel when a person is listening to his/her words?

- How does one feel when a person is not listening to his/her words?

- Why is it sometimes difficult to listen? What does it mean to *actively* listen?

- Why is listening important?

STOP LISTENING!

As a method of truly emphasizing the importance of listening, ask a student to speak to you about an important topic. Encourage the participant to choose a topic that is recent, significant, and known to everyone in the room. Role-play the "non-listener," the individual who makes minimal efforts, sounds and gestures, in an effort to persuade the speaker to believe that he or she is listening. When the speaker begins engaging the topic, behave in somewhat the following manner: Eyes moving quickly from side to side, head turning, glancing at your wristwatch or the wall clock, continually nodding, shuffling papers on your desk, repeating "Yep, yep," and with little if any real eye contact.

Following the verbal attempt, ask the speaker how he or she feels about your reaction. "Left out, not important, unsuccessful, like you didn't care about me or what I had to say."

Then ask the individual to engage in delivering the message again. This time hold still, leaning forward, maintaining eye contact, nodding from time to time, and using verbal "cultural fillers," (I see / really! / hard to believe! / no kidding! as well as facial responses). Once again, ask how the speaker feels. I'm sure you can easily anticipate the dissimilar reaction. Emphasize the importance of listening; we all need to do it. Can we all improve?

Yes!

B. A LISTENING ACTIVITY:

At this point, the teacher may introduce the skills to employ when practicing the art of successful listening. Techniques and approaches are discussed earlier in chapter 7. (Not only can a teacher benefit from utilizing the procedure; students may gain, as well.)

Skills to be covered:

Reflective Listening   **Summarizing**
Paraphrasing   **Avoid Barriers to Communication**

(Definitions and methods of usage are available in chapter 7)

After covering the above skills, instruct the class to develop a two- or three-minute message to verbally share with a classmate. The message could be based upon almost anything—opinions, events, sports, future plans in life. Then, explain the strategies found on the next page (listener and speaker responsibilities), while demonstrating how to engage them. Students should, of course, be given sufficient time to study the task in preparing.

Divide the kids into groups of two, a speaker and a listener. Following three-to five-minute engagements, instruct each of the two to feed back to the other - thoughts, feelings, and observations concerning the exchange along with what was heard. What transpired? How did it succeed? Following that, reverse the roles. Or, have a duo go through the activity in the center of the room. Then, review the experience using comments from the entire class.

Listener

Focusing	Attending	Reaction
-Finds a purpose for listening.	-Decides whether message is organized.	-Asks for further clarification.
-Is prepared to deal with major distractions	-Tries to anticipate speaker's point(s) - accepts or rejects them	-Feeds back major points
-Is ready and willing to be attentive	-Asks for clarification	-Voices concerns constructively
-Attempts to be open-minded	-Evaluates Remains sensitive to non-verbal messages	

Speaker

Focusing	Attending	Reaction
-Prepares message with a purpose.	-Presents message in a clear and organized manner.	-Accepts and responds to questions.

-Decides what to say and how to say it.	-Speaks clearly with appropriate volume and speed.	-Is sensitive to listener's reaction.
-Feels free to use non-verbal communication.	-Is open to constructive criticism.	

Processing the Listening activity can also help promote a better understanding of time spent. This is the same approach used earlier in this chapter.

- "Why do you think I introduced the lesson?"

- "What did you learn?"

- "What surprised you?"

- "What kind of student would really like this activity?"

- "What would you change in the activity to make the lesson better?"

- "How are you feeling about what we just did?"

Conclude by describing any significant behaviors you observed.

C. THE NEXT STEP: WHAT STOPS SOME STUDENTS FROM BECOMING ENTHUSIASTICALLY ENGAGED IN A CLASS ACTIVITY?

The following activity includes all lesson details used in its development. I suggest initially reading it in its entirety.
A "Lesson plan" version, exists within the appendix – <u>Lesson #3b</u>)

Where do we go from here? Engage in a lesson where the pupils discuss common difficulties that occur when an individual is simply not working up to his or her potential. On occasions, we've all noticed when certain kids are reluctant to participate in class activities. Can these problems be addressed? Without question!

Additionally, the students will see evidence of the teacher's fairness, patience, understanding, and *respect*.

Positive communication / Active listening / Working up to potential – - all work together in increasing academic success.

Introduce and pursue the following topics. During the student interaction, perhaps walk the room observing examples of students' use of the Listening Skills.

1. What is it about *others* that stops me from becoming enthusiastically engaged in a class activity?

- Individual responses on paper. Grammar and spelling do *not* apply.

- Discussion with a partner. Share, discuss, make suggestions.

- Time permitting: Discussion in groups of four. Share, discuss, make suggestions.

- Class discussion in a Community Meeting.

- Instruct participants to silently write Prescriptions (this technique was introduced in chapter 6), making suggestions to help deal with the concerns shared earlier by classmates.

- The teacher or a student reads the responses, or the teacher hands them out to appropriate students in need of suggestive help. Further discussions at discretion of teacher and class.

RATIONALE:

It gives students an opportunity to:

- See evidence of others' frustration ("I'm not the only one....").

- Relieve some of *their* frustration.

- Discover solutions to some of their problems.

- See evidence of teacher's fairness, patience, understanding, and respect.

2. What is it about *me* that stops me from becoming enthusiastically engaged in a class activity?

<u>Follow same process</u>: Individual responses, discussion with partner, groups of four, class Community Meeting discussion, Prescriptions.

It is important for students to understand why, on occasion, they may not "feel like" becoming involved in small or large-group activities. Their reluctance is sometimes caused by those with whom they work, while at other times it may be caused by their own views and moods. Are they aware of this? Possibly not. In either case, steps can be taken to better understand and counter-act the problem.[7]

Processing the activity above could be quite helpful.

———

Is the problem always caused by the kids? Is it sometimes caused by the school environment, professionals, schedules, educational demands? – Without question! One successful way of gaining better support from students is by giving them a measure of involvement in designing the academic environment and routine of daily lessons. Consider the following activity.

———

ACTIVITY #3: DEVELOPING THE CLASSROOM CONTRACT

The following activity includes all lesson details used in its development. I suggest initially reading it in its entirety. A "lesson plan" version, exists within the appendix –Lesson #3c

Today's students learn a great deal from adults who *model* appropriate behavior as well as engage the classroom instruction of it. Consequently, when dealing with adolescents, it is crucial for teachers to consider several important factors. Your pupils need to be consistently treated with honesty, compassion, patience and respect, (as well as proper discipline when necessary). A good teacher will also come to realize that his or her students need to be somewhat empowered. It is immensely beneficial if the kids feel as though they have some control over their academic and social lives on a daily basis.

Some individuals who feel totally at the mercy of others' authority stand a lesser chance of experiencing as strong a sense of motivation, of sustaining sincere commitment, and consequently, of attaining lasting academic success. Allowing students to have a measure of control over their daily affairs strongly increases the chances of boosting their self-confidence and optimism, thus motivating them to take positive educational risks.

Addressing the self-esteem of one's students should be a goal of every teacher. When we meet our students, at some stage of adolescence, personalities are not totally developed. Rather, their personal growth is ongoing and continues to be affected by life's experiences. As teachers, we can provide an atmosphere that will allow self-esteem to grow and prosper. The results among adolescents are greater self-confidence, a more satisfying educational experience, increased academic performance, fewer absences, and increased morale. Additionally, I believe other benefits could very well be a reduction in vandalism, a rejection of substance abuse, and even abstinence from risky sexual behavior. I see these "reductions" as potential results of improved self-confidence and self-esteem.

What better way of boosting confidence and creating a positive classroom environment than through the use of a *Contract*.

At this point, your pupils can help develop the classroom's "rules and daily routine" for the coming year by constructing an agreement with the teacher. Students retain far more from their active *involvement* in an activity than from a traditional teacher-led session. The goal is to guarantee a more enjoyable, increasingly successful academic experience.

The teacher could begin with something like, "As we've pointed out, one thing that may prevent a student from enthusiastically participating in a class activity could be behavior on the part of one or more of the other students; or it could be something that lives within the student himself/herself. Additionally, however, it could honestly be something that exists within the school environment or daily lessons, as well. I'd like to talk about this for a while.

"In the past, have you taken courses that seemed unappealing, absent of any enjoyment and true academic creativity—just not what you might have been hoping for? Yeah, I know, more than likely. Have you taken courses that were just the opposite—courses that you actually enjoyed? Yes, it does make a difference.

"Well, I'd like to do whatever I can to make this course one you'll remember in a positive way. In order to help us move in that direction, I'd like to develop a contract with you. As some of you may know, a contract represents two sides that come together to construct an agreement. What do you want to get out of my class this year? What are you hoping to gain?"

With that, ask them to brainstorm (described below) a list of **"Gets,"** perhaps on newsprint, screen, or front board, that reflect the type of attainments they wish to derive in your course. (These "Gets" may pertain to the curriculum or the general classroom environment and routine)

————

Brainstorming: Students are encouraged to vocally state a response to a question, statement, or situation. No raising of hands is required. All responses are accepted and recorded in full view of the entire group on a board or newsprint. This encourages total involvement in a discussion and is very time-efficient. They are asked to refrain from private, one-on-one conversations. (Some may be asked to repeat their suggestions if not clearly heard by the teacher)

Withhold analyzing or questioning any of the submissions as this may dampen enthusiasm and some individuals might not actively engage in the activity. Responses may be evaluated at the conclusion of the activity.

Ask for clarification only where necessary, being careful not to put students in a position where they must defend their contributions. This activity worked very well, allowing me to save considerable time.

- All brainstormed ideas are valid, accepted, and written down.

- Most will be reasonable. Those that are not can be dealt with later.

Some common Gets often suggested by students: Help with homework after school, individual help with the skill of writing, good grades, positive notes to parents, extra credit opportunities, homework passes, write all assignments in clear view and leave them there for several days, read novels that students select, spend time reading silently in class, go on field trips.

Following the brainstorming, approach any suggestions that are unusable:

(Have Friday afternoons off, play in the gym every morning, eat lunch daily in the classroom.) In approaching the unusable suggestions, you could recognize those that would be unattainable or you could ask class members to identify any proposals that might be difficult or impossible.

- For example, point out that "Friday afternoons off" would be frowned upon by the principal, superintendent, board of education, parents, etc... impossible. According to state law, it's also illegal. "Are there any other brainstormed items that would be difficult or impossible to attain and therefore, a waste of time in pursuing?" Allow students time to identify them and ask their permission to eliminate those strongly unlikely to be accepted.

- You could suggest substituting something else. Rather than having Fridays off, perhaps use part of one class each semester to celebrate a holiday. Write it down.

- Additionally, your own schedule would not allow you to eat in the room on a daily basis, but would you be willing to arrange it once or twice during the course of the year?

- Making these types of concessions can display your willingness to work with the class and construct a meaningful Contract.

Next, disclose a prepared list of your additional contributions—your "Gives":

- Time and energy

- Teach to the best of my ability

- Knowledge

- Respect

- Friendship

- Patience

- Humor

Perhaps offer **The Early Bird Special** described in chapter 6.

...and finally, a last "Give" possibly similar to one of the following- Go on a hike, go swimming, have a dance, have a picnic...—something absolutely chosen by the teacher to get their attention while driving home the unique quality of <u>the Contract</u>. As a surprise, I used to uncover a sheet of newsprint hanging on the wall with the words, "Go swimming at the Canajoharie Pool!" And, "Stop at McDonald's on the way home." They were in disbelief; they loved it! Needless to say, the contract made a major influence.

Disclose another list of, "Non negotiables." Try not to make it too long. Examples:

- No violence.

- No put-downs or bullying.

- No lying.

At this point, they may brainstorm their list of Gives to Get:

"Take a look at your list of Gets. Now, what are you willing to give *me* in order to attain them?" What are they willing to *Give* so as to receive their list of *Gets*? If, in your view, certain necessary class <u>Gives</u> are not suggested by students (homework on time, punctual arrival, good study habits, etc.), ask that they put themselves in your position for a moment; what would they ask for if they were a teacher in charge of instruction? Or, if necessary, you could simply make a request.

Finally, review all brainstormed items.

This activity establishes a climate of cooperation within the room. It also utilizes positive peer pressure in keeping fellow students on task and conscientiously committed to success. And, of course, it's <u>unconventional.</u>

If a student, perhaps, finds difficulty in cooperating in some way, you may initiate a <u>private</u> contract with only that individual. This approach allows room for negotiation while leaving the student's dignity intact. We need to remember how influential our behavior can be with these young people. Treating them with dignity not only generates greater potential for the development of their self-worth; it also models appropriate behavior, which can frequently sustain positive relationships within their group of peers and with the teacher.

Out of the eighteen years during which I developed a contract with several classes per year, only once did I have to dissolve it. In a non-threatening way, I explained my reasons, then threw out the document. I waited a few days, and sure enough, two kids approached me asking to consider negotiating again. If they hadn't approached me, I would have eventually found a way to bring the word "contract" back into a classroom discussion myself.

"What if"... If one or two students didn't abide by an existing contract, I could have asked them, as well as the class as a whole, if they preferred that the individuals simply not participate. If there were few Gives on the part of the non-participating pupils, they would receive few Gets. There would be no discernible grudges; that would simply be the way it would be. That situation, however, never arose.[8]

CHAPTER 9: THE SEAT OF DISTINCTION:

(The following activity includes all lesson details used in its development. I suggest initially reading it in its entirety. A "lesson plan" version, exists within the appendix – <u>Lesson #4</u>)

THE NEXT STEP: CONTINUE IMPROVING THE COOPERATIVE ENVIRONMENT

Their behavior, at times, can be erratic, concerning, confusing, infuriating, offensive. We know this. It doesn't mean, however, that we should sit idly by as it occurs, without intervening. And most certainly, we must not ignore acts of bullying **or** self-disapproval among these young people. Increasingly, more educational professionals identify the school setting as a potential source of coercion for our students—to some extent academically, but certainly socially. Though it is a necessary and healthy practice to hold students accountable for taking on scholastic challenges, we must also keep in mind that we work with impressionable young minds that are frequently exposed to social intimidation and even physical threats emanating from their peers. These potential sources of bullying (authentic or imagined) often serve to alienate our young and cause them to withdraw from social and, subsequently, academic endeavors. Additionally, there exist more grievous results of social harassment within society such as physical injury to oneself, harm to others, and even suicide.

Many of these youngsters require help in recognizing that most adolescents have similar concerns and uncertainties about peer interaction. One major uncertainty they have: How does a kid go about successfully dealing with fellow students on a daily basis? I believe they can be made to clearly understand that there are no "winners" when insults are hurled at one another, and that everyone comes out ahead when support and empathy are used within the classroom environment. There are methods to promote a greater sensitivity to the feelings of others and thereby create more positive relationships among classmates. Likewise, pointless *self*-criticism can also lead to an unhealthy pattern of behavior, which, in the long run, may negatively affect a student's academic performance as well as physical well-being.

Many teachers believe that the school arena can actually be used as a venue within which students may take a closer look at the challenges described above. Peer criticism, too often a major problem, can be a frequent occurrence. With the use of the following technique, this challenge can be affected. Class members can discuss a social problem, analyze it, and ultimately reduce its affect.

When the "Seat of Distinction" is employed, the kids themselves are directly involved in developing a solution to the "put-down concern." With direct involvement, kids retain the inspiration motivated by the activity for a longer period of time. The following session encourages sensitivity to the feelings of others *and* reinforces the students' positive attitudes about themselves, thereby reducing the possibility of self-deprecation.

-Sensitivity to feelings of peers + reduction of self-deprecation = less bullying, more environmental comfort, and greater academic success-

Hence, success within the realm of education is encouraged and improved.

I. THE SEAT OF DISTINCTION (BUILDING A LEVEL OF TRUST AND COMFORT AMONG STUDENTS, ALONG WITH INVOLVEMENT OF THE TEACHER)

A. This activity can provide opportunities for students to engage in honest communication, encouraging peer acceptance and bonding, while discouraging injuries to pride and egos through bullying or any other inappropriate behavior.

1. The lesson encourages the opening of valuable lines of communication, promoting tolerance, understanding, and the reality that everyone possesses valuable qualities. It, additionally, promotes the reality that we experience similar needs, and our treatment of classmates strongly affects their feelings and self-esteem.
2. It provides students with opportunities to experience sincere complimentary messages from peers who would, in all probability, not have taken the time to express those positive thoughts if not involved in this activity.

B. Students will demonstrate, personally and socially, responsible behaviors. They will display respect for themselves and others.

PURPOSES OF THE LESSON

- To open positive lines of communication

- To enhance self-esteem

- To give class members opportunities to offer and hear sincere complimentary messages

- To practice accepting sincere compliments without an attempt to deflect them

- To address the ramifications of pointless criticism and bullying

- To demonstrate our common needs

- To reduce or eliminate self-disapproval

- To break barriers and enhance relationships

- To underscore the reality that every classmate possesses positive qualities

II. PROCEDURE

A. Role-play an example of strong criticism with a student who's been made aware of the lesson's objective and has consented to taking part in the role-play. (Other students are to be made aware of the role-play).

Example, with voice somewhat raised:

"Bruce, you've forgotten your homework again! You'll never learn! You're nothing more than a failure! Why can't you be more like Mary?"

B. Then, direct the students' attention to a Smartboard or drop a rolled sheet of newsprint that reads: "<u>What may the result be if a person frequently hears severe criticism?</u>"—making the class aware that it was a role-play. (Aside: "Nice going, Bruce. We had them believing it.")

C. Have the class brainstorm responses to the question. Examples: "He'll feel dumb." "She'll really begin to believe it." "He'll have little self-confidence." "She'll withdraw, not do well in school, not want to participate, want to do harm to herself." Display the printed responses in the front of the room.

D. Discuss. On newsprint, Smartboard, etc.: "<u>What's it easier to do, criticize or compliment someone?</u>" (Obviously, criticize.)

   1. As an example, ask students to raise their hands if they can think of two or three compliments they can direct toward the school cafeteria. Then, following a short discussion, ask for two or three critical comments. (Which were easier to attain?) <u>We can always criticize.</u> *It's easy.*

E. Discuss: "Why is it that when we are genuinely impressed by one's behavior, we seldom communicate that impression to him or her?" (Be patient with their responses if there are more than expected.)

F. Discuss: "How do you feel when someone says something <u>nice</u> about you?" (Good, embarrassed, worthwhile, weird, cool,...)

G. "Why is it that when we receive compliments, we sometimes deflect the praise?

   1. "I think you did a great job during the volley ball game on Saturday."

"Well, we lost. I should have been able to serve much more effectively." (What does this tell us about our ability to accept compliments?)

All one really needs to say is, "Thank you." Additionally, when we deflect a compliment, the <u>complimentor</u> may feel that his or her comment has been discounted and therefore is being ignored.

The above introduction initiates several discussions on its own. Consequently, it may easily take a full period, or even longer, to complete. It is beneficial, however, if students are totally focused upon the theme.

H. Instructions: The Seat of Distinction: Explain that each class member will have the opportunity to receive positive messages from classmates when sitting in "The Chair."

<u>Ground rules</u>:

   1. All compliments must be of a sincere and honest nature; they must deal with p.ersonal achievements or qualities, not with appearance. ("I like your sneakers.")

   2. The chair occupant may not respond to messages in any way other than saying, "Thank you," if so inclined. This prevents students from deflecting a compliment; they must accept it.

I. Appoint five students to collectively sit apart from the class, perhaps on the side of the room. These people make up the "Praising Panel." Their responsibility is to share sincere, positive messages with the chair's occupants. The teacher should encourage members of the Praising Panel to call the occupant by name and maintain eye contact. This personalizes the praise and allows it to be sincerely "felt" more keenly by the student sitting in The Chair.

1. Demonstrate by complimenting a student while not facing him or her and then again while maintaining eye contact. Ask which time the compliment felt more meaningful. The student may elaborate.

2. Caution members of the Praising Panel to begin thinking of an honest compliment as soon as they know who will be occupying The Seat of Distinction. In this way, youngsters will not suddenly find themselves unprepared to share a sincere word of kindness. "I can't think of anything" is certainly counterproductive.

J. Other members of the class may then follow the panel with additional positive messages.

K. At conclusion, ask the occupant of The Chair:

1. "How was the experience?" If the student responds, "Embarrassing!"…ask, "Embarrassing-Good or embarrassing-Bad? Weird-Good, or Weird-Bad?" etc..

Ask students to clarify when necessary.

2. Ask the occupant, "Did you hear anything that you didn't expect to hear? (Share them or pass.) Though peers may not frequently offer positive comments to each other, they more than likely *do* have thoughts of praise for their classmates, and it's worthwhile taking the opportunity to vocally offer them. Drive this home.

3. Finally, ask the departing seat occupant, "Who'll be the next classmate to occupy the 'Seat of Distinction?'"

L. After the student in the chair selects the next occupant, he or she taps a member of the Praising Panel out and replaces that individual as a "complimentor."

M. Closure: When all have occupied the chair, promote a discussion held during a Community Meeting. Possibly refer to the purposes of the lesson (found under I. B).

Processing this event, as described in the section on the Milling Assassin, helps promote an even better understanding.

III. ASSESSMENT TOOLS AND TECHNIQUES:

A. Following the experience, continue to listen for daily exchanges that reflect the main points of the lesson. With the student's permission, perhaps bring them to the class's attention. Students' intentions should be to offer comments that:

- demonstrate respect for themselves and others.

- demonstrate personal and social responsible behaviors.

- acknowledge the benefits of accepting praise from peers.

- express the idea that deflecting compliments serves no one's best interest.

- acknowledge our common needs for acceptance.

- recognize that ways in which peers are treated may affect one's feelings, self-confidence, and academic and social success.

- identify the need for tolerance, understanding, and empathy.

- reflect the idea that when complimentary thoughts occur, they should most often be <u>expressed</u>.

- accept the idea that compliments "feel good" to the complimentor as well as the person being praised.

- acknowledge that it's very easy to criticize.

B. Prior to the Community Meeting, students may pair up in twos or fours and discuss the experience by applying active listening skills. Possibly assign an essay on The Seat of Distinction.

D. Observe the social interaction of your pupils to determine the impression made by the activity.

E. Students may discuss behavior changes observed that they believe can be attributed to experiencing the lesson.

IV. REFLECTION

- It may be advantageous to have earlier exposed the class to any lessons and/or experiences (including videos or speakers) addressing "put-downs," tolerance, compassion, diversity, fairness, and unnecessary criticism before initiating <u>The Seat of Distinction</u>. These experiences help set the stage for the activity, reduce possible intimidation, and promote a greater level of comfort with the teacher.

———

TESTIMONY

At one point in my career, I contacted a group of older students who had experienced The Seat of Distinction years earlier. I asked if they remembered the activity and if they would respond to a question based upon the lesson.

(On occasion, the activity was also called "The Hot Seat.")

The question, simply stated, was: "What do you remember about an activity within which you participated while a sixth-grader called The Seat of Distinction?"

RESPONSES FROM PARTICIPANTS (ABSOLUTELY UNALTERED)

Kate: I enjoyed the Hot Seat. When I was in the hot seat, I felt many things, but everything I felt was good. I felt embarrassed, comforted, liked, excited, thoughtful, warm, wanted, and useful. The hot seat gives a boost of confidence. I think the hot seat is a wonderful idea.

Tammy: Thinking back to sixth grade, there are many memories. The "hot Seat" stood out to me because it changed the way I thought of myself and other students. By sharing only positive comments with each other, the students, including myself, really began to feel better about themselves. I know that I, personally, realized that I have many great qualities that, perhaps, I was overlooking. Too many children focus on the negative qualities they "think" they have. Maybe that has to do with being at "that awkward age." The "Hot Seat" made me realize what a good person I really was on the inside.

Bobby: There are many reasons the "Hot Seat" was important to me. When I was in the Hot Seat, I felt happy because the people were telling me my good qualities. I also felt good when I was on the Praising Panel because then, I got to see how happy they were because I was telling them about their good qualities.

A PARENT'S RESPONSE

Diane: As a parent of one of Mr. Sgambato's students, and as a fellow colleague, I recall him describing this activity at our parent orientation night and thinking what a wonderful lesson to help foster self-esteem and positive relationships among students.

I recall my daughter relating to us how difficult it was for her to sit in the "Hot Seat" and hear her friends say positive things and give her compliments, but also how "strange and wonderful she felt inside." She enjoyed sitting on the Praising Panel and having the opportunity to give her friends compliments where she would not be ostracized for doing so.

In a time of their development where put-downs and criticisms are seen as "cool" behavior, it was refreshing for me as an educator and a parent to see how one teacher was striving to encourage positiveness and compliments among these young people. I thought this was an *excellent* lesson and opportunity!

SECTION FOUR:

IS THERE MORE THAT WE CAN DO?

CHAPTER 10: ACTION FEVER

Positive, meaningful endeavors sometime arise as a result of seemingly insignificant beginnings.

This one began just before lunch as my students and I waited in line to pick up our trays. Two sixth-grade girls were complaining about there being so little for them to do in our small, rural township. As the complaints continued, several more students joined in the conversation. Soon, as you might expect, one of the kids turned to me and asked, "Mr. Sgambato, what can we do for fun in our free time?"

I briefly searched my mind, then described some of the things I'd done during my earlier life. They tried to be polite, but it was very apparent that building soapbox cars and playing touch football were not what they were looking for. The encounter, however, got me thinking, and at the beginning of the following week, I invited the group of kids to my room during a study hall.

I made my proposal: "What if we organized a group of sixth graders to continue pursuing this discussion, to talk about what eleven and twelve year old kids can do for enjoyment? How can you kids have some fun? Also, how about looking around the school, our neighborhoods, and our town to see what we can do that might improve things in our village? Are there senior citizens that could use a hand with cleaning, shoveling, errands? Could local organizations use assistance? I think that situations around here can be developed. We can have some fun, and…we can *make a difference*."

The response was a chorus of affirmatives. Now, they happened to be all girls, but that didn't mean the guys wouldn't be interested. So, on the following day, our morning announcements included a description of the new group being organized, plus the time and location of the first meeting. I mentioned it in all my classes, put signs up in the halls, and asked the group of young ladies to talk it up among their friends.

At the end of the following day, the number of attendees was surprising; in fact, there weren't enough chairs in my room. Many had to sit on top of desks or stand in the back of the room. My proposition was this: They were welcome to meet in my room on a weekly basis to discuss ideas relating to any activities they wished to initiate. Additionally, they could brainstorm a list of things they might consider pursuing that would make the school and the local area simply better. Some of the results are listed:

Things to do for fun	Things to do for the area
Go camping	Collect money for in a cancer drive
Have a Halloween dance	Clean up areas of town
Go roller skating	Hold a raffle to raise money for the needy
Go swimming	Hold a bake sale to raise money for the needy
Go on a hike	Help the elderly in any way we can
	Babysit for parents attending teacher conferences—

As we were organizing, I asked the kids to consider a name for our newly formed group. A young lady by the name of Kim suggested, "Action Fever." The more I thought about it, the more it seemed to fit our intentions and personalities. Apparently, the kids saw it the same way; they adopted the name and we went into action. What was to be our first step?

We decided to clearly identify our goals and begin our adventures. After discussing the concept at length with those interested, I produced the following declaration:

ACTION FEVER

Goals:

A. To attempt to affect the school, the kids, and the community in positive ways—to improve the climate and make things better.

B. To make ourselves feel good doing things that we enjoy doing.

C. To inspire individuals to increase self-confidence and build trust between themselves and members of our community.

D. To encourage opportunities for us to meet with success.

E. To work on leadership skills to be used in school and in life.

As we ventured through the projects and activities, word spread. Seventh- and eighth-graders approached me in an effort to join. "How come it's limited to just the sixth grade? We go to school here, too."

You're ahead of me, no doubt. How could I say no? There were soon nearly fifty members. "I can help out sixth period." "I'm free after school, Mr. Sgambato." "Can I come to school early tonight?" They approached project after project. All they needed was a little push, a suggestion, an arm around a shoulder, and a nod. Each individual supplied the necessary energy.

As far as the suggested projects and activities listed, we did them *all*— yes, we did. The group actually went on two hikes and held several dances. We raised nearly $300 for the Cancer Fund, $235 for a local family that suffered a fire, and $423 just from our first two dances. We had our treasury. It did take a deal of planning, reaching out to administrators, service organizations, parents, bus drivers, and the local paper. The kids were committed, however, and, therefore, so was I.

The most stirring, benevolent, and charitable endeavor was something called, Project HELP: Help the Elderly by Lending People. We visited the town's senior citizen center and explained our idea. From local ministers, Meals on Wheels, and Social Services, we acquired the names of older individuals who were in need of having chores done or errands run. We then contacted the individuals, making them aware of our services, and asked if our people could be of any help (free of charge). After the chore was performed or the errand run, the Action Fever member would report his or her progress to me. Finally, I made a follow-up contact with the community member to review any successes or flaws that had possibly occurred. Problems were to be addressed by the group. There were <u>none</u>. Project HELP resulted in greater pride and self-esteem experienced by the students, along with a strong message to our senior citizens that these kids cared.

Hey, they're just kids. Yes, that is what we call them; that is how they are labeled.

They *are* kids; however, kids that can be determined, eager, generous, and conscientious. When given the opportunity to help, they *are* resourceful, successful, and happy to be involved. Do encounters such as these help mold them? Of course. Through their repeated exposures to these types of activities, they come to realize just how beneficial and valuable they can be, (to the **recipient** as well as the **provider**). This proved to be one of the most wonderfully emotional events experienced during my teaching career.

CHAPTER 11: SUPPORT GROUPS FOR ADOLESCENTS

Kids fighting. School shootings. Teenagers tragically taking their own lives.

The media continues to highlight the violent responses to struggles and dilemmas existing within the lives of some of our young people. The more often kids become aware of these reactions, the more easily some may sadly come to consider them.

Too frequently, society does not teach juveniles how to resolve conflicts; they are taught, regrettably, to retaliate, or to totally give up. (...and to some, it, unfortunately, appears a viable alternative to pursue). Consequently, the weight of catastrophic events such as these will hover within affected families forever.

As Americans, we quietly sit, staring at the horror on our TV screens while indulging in immense sadness and displaying expressions of misery and grief.

"What can I do? I'm only one person."

What can you do? What can *we* do? --*Something!* We must begin constructing an approach to the problem.

Ultimately, concerned Americans must lock arms, initiating a movement toward resolving this increasing threat of violence among our nation's young. We need to become *involved*. The longer society waits to react, the greater the possibility that attention will drift and the less likely we'll be to begin moving strongly in a positive direction.

Like so many others, the tragic increase in teen violence, over the last few years, has greatly affected me. To help, I can only offer something learned from my career in education. It may not be the ultimate, complete answer, but is, I believe, a *piece* of the puzzle...an effective piece; even a *proactive* piece: *Support Groups.*

Though extreme violent behavior, thankfully, does *not* enter the lives of the majority of adolescents, they too must deal, from time to time, with emotional predicaments and dilemmas (confusion, discomfort, depression, anger). Consequently, support groups could offer many of our kids a measure of reassurance, comfort, and encouragement.

These young folks are growing, changing, emerging—without a doubt, a difficult stage for some to experience. Disagreements with friends and parents, problems with schoolwork, and comments from teachers may occasionally result in unexpected, negative, emotional responses. As their personalities begin to develop a sense of identity, they more easily become confused, anxious, depressed, angry—and cannot always identify the cause, nor how to deal with the emotion. Some are on the verge of entering adulthood, and I believe that this transition is more difficult today than ever before. To whom do our kids talk to when in need...feeling lost, bullied, intimidated, insecure, or just overwhelmed by life?

We would prefer to say, Mom and Dad. That would be a comfortable conclusion; kids approaching their loving parents for advice, support, affection, and confidential disclosure. However, my thirty-five year career and my confidential conversations with many students have convinced me that, the majority of the time, adolescents do *not* divulge fears, confusion, emotional struggles, love interests, or other encountered difficulties to parents. They may, occasionally reach out to a teacher or a friend, but far too frequently, the problem remains unassisted, suppressed, and consequently, increases in its severity.

The majority of kids, judging from my experience, <u>internalize</u> the problem. Consequently, this can lead to greater complications. How does it affect their comfort, relationships, attitude, personality, sense of trust, education, and future? Will anger set in and could **violence** result?

One way to help our kids through these challenging times is in forming student **support groups**. I'm not implying, however, that anyone and everyone in the teaching profession can nor should take on this project. You may not wish to tread into areas where you do not feel comfortable, or you may not have the support of the administration, the board of education, or even your colleagues in entering the world of private and personal student struggles. However, if the venture <u>can</u> be approached, and you are interested, please read on.

This concept targets a vulnerable age group introducing the kids to a protected setting where they may begin interacting and building trust. The sessions are organized in an effort to give the youths a forum within which to express, explore, and better understand ensuing emotions. Within the group, they may come to realize that they are not alone in suffering misgivings and reservations. Students attending such gatherings can learn more about the world of adolescence while acquiring new skills to deal with personal concerns. End result: The development of greater self-assurance.

In time, they become aware of similar concerns existing in the lives of other group members as well as how they are perceived by their peers. Thus, they may gain measured confidence. With greater assurance acquired, they can develop and practice new behaviors, and thus better understand how to deal with the many problems life can present during this potentially threatening period. In the twelve years that I offered opportunities for participants to meet, only twice did I receive a parental permission slip opting not to include a pupil. And only once did a student decide, after a few weeks, to drop out of the sessions. His reason for the action was that he "...didn't need it." I actually agreed with his decision.

FACILITATOR

Now, how does a classroom teacher prepare to take on the role of a group facilitator? The truth is that I don't have a simple answer. In my opinion, however, one must feel comfortable with the challenge to be undertaken and make a sincere vow to seek advice from appropriate professionals when necessary.

How would the facilitator go about developing an approach and final plan? First of all, it would be best if anyone interested in facilitating did his or her own research, possibly interviewing the professionals for advice: School psychologists, clinical psychologists, guidance counselors, the principal, and the superintendent.

Would a course in adolescent psychology be helpful? I did take an adolescent psych course, which, in fact, did prove to be somewhat useful. However, I believe that the most powerful driving force in developing a successful approach to help group members was my *desire to make things better* for them. If that is the chief motivator for you, as well, I trust that you are truly in the right frame of mind, moving in the right direction. Of primary importance: Sincere concern: They need someone to *listen* (and, of course, to care). OK, so, where can you begin?

Progress can be made in reading available material from appropriate texts or tapping into the abundant information accessible online. Additionally, as mentioned earlier, there is nothing wrong with reaching out to professionals within the field of psychology in acquiring methods of approaching the task. Would any nearby professional be willing to offer you a short session or personal advice based upon adolescent support group management? Then again, who knows these kids best? You're around them nearly 200 days a year. You've observed them, scolded them, laughed with them, spoken one-on-one with them…. They trust you. Aren't you a valuable professional?

In preparing the young members of my support groups within the school environment, I explained very honestly that I might not be qualified to answer all questions and would possibly "pass" if they inquired about subjects of which I knew little. The facilitator can certainly put an answer to a question on hold until the next session. There would be time, therefore, to contact a qualified individual from whom to confidentially obtain pertinent information, which I did on several occasions. You are obviously **not** the psychological expert; you are the **teacher** who is giving your students an opportunity to speak, to vent, to share, to help. There is, however, a limit as to what you can provide. Additionally, it would be proper to inform the members that confidentiality would be absolute on your part—unless, of course, you become aware of potentially physical (or mental) harm to any individual. ***In that case, you would be obligated to speak out and properly seek appropriate help for the individual(s) involved.*** Referring the young people to professionals may be, at times, the only option. These professional individuals providing additional help would be **any** experts having the authority to prevent physical or mental harm to anyone.

We can assume, the administration, or perhaps, the board of education, would most likely have to give you their blessings before you take on the responsibility.

WHAT PERSONALITY TRAITS WOULD HELP MAKE A SUCCESSFUL FACILITATOR?

In my opinion, the facilitator would need to be proficient at:

- Seeing the world through the eyes of an adolescent.

- Being perceptive; able to read a kid's facial expression and body language, assessing the "slow walk, tipped head," interpreting eye contact (or lack of it).

- Anticipating certain moods or personality traits based upon how students maneuver, speak (volume and intensity) and physically carry themselves.

- Using emotional intelligence—being aware of one's own emotions, as well as recognizing emotions in others and responding appropriately.

- Having a good rapport with kids.

- Having an active sense of humor.

- Being considerably patient.

- Having respect for one's students.

WHAT CAN THE GROUP PROVIDE?

The group can provide an environment within which students may express their genuine feelings, discuss ensuing emotional issues, build self-confidence, self-esteem, and deal honestly with peers, as well as gather pride and satisfaction when <u>being of help to other members</u>. Participants may more clearly see their own positive purposes in life.

- Through group sessions, participants can learn to better understand and deal with their own insecurities as they discover that most of their peers often experience similar confusion, discomfort, annoyance, and uncertainties.

- These young people can be encouraged to voice opinions, seek answers, and deal honestly with themselves and others.

- They attain the crucial gratification of having others quietly and sincerely listen to their problems without interruption.

- The more often a member hears innermost revelations expressed by a peer, the more likely the member is to reveal his or her own most personal concerns.

- Students, through open dialogue, may come to better understand fellow classmates (as well as themselves).

- Within the protected setting, they are free to bounce ideas off other members whenever feeling the motivation.

- The setting also offers pupils the opportunity to display their authentic empathy for other members. In helping fellow members, they more easily experience gratification, pride, and self-respect while realizing their potential value to others.

- They may develop the realization that they each possess the capability to come to a friend's aid in offering useful coping strategies as well as sincere support.

- With time and commitment, they can easily conclude that peers in the group do care about them, and they may come to value their support.

- Here, they have the opportunity to truly be themselves, saying whatever they wish to say in whatever way they wish to say it.

Additionally, with support, they may determine a way to better avoid:
- Feelings of insecurity.

- Dwindling self-esteem.

- Anger in solitude.

- The danger of resorting to **violence** as a remedy in solving problems and insecurities.

My method was to identify the kids that would very likely benefit from such an experience and approach them in a friendly, unorthodox manner, one or two at a time. I would explain that I was starting a cool group which would meet twice a week to listen to and confidentially discuss problems that members might be experiencing. Participants would be able to trust each other. Those attending would be free to talk about any difficulty being encountered for whatever length of time necessary, and explain it in whatever way they wished. If time ran out, they could continue during the next session. When approaching the majority of perspective members, I made it a point not to sound as though I thought he/she **needed** help. I was simply offering it to a *few* of my students. It was the offer of an opportunity that they were free to accept or refuse.

I called the group, Teen Rap. Rapping would be considered talking, and the inclusion of the term, *teen*, frankly was my ploy to have them consider the assemblage as something an older group of kids might take part in. The implication: They would be treated as though they were older... teenagers, in fact. Consequently, I believe they attempted to adopt what they considered to be a more mature attitude.

The following directions were passed out to all group members:

TEEN-RAP OUTLINE
You may

- Express your feelings about anything.

- Get to know others in the group better.

- Get to know yourself better.

- Bounce ideas off the other members.

- Say whatever you wish in whatever manner you wish.

- Be certain that all would be kept confidential.

———

My letter to the parents:

Adolescents often experience events during the course of the school day which trigger discomfort and difficulty. Disagreements with friends, problems with school work, or even comments from teachers may result in negative emotional responses on the part of numerous students. One method of helping our kids through these difficult times is forming <u>support groups</u>.

Student support groups are organized in an effort to give the youths a forum within which to express, explore, and understand common emotions. Students can learn new skills, develop self-confidence, and become more aware of how others view them. They can practice newly learned responses, and better understand how to deal with the many problems life presents. Additionally, they can gather pride and satisfaction in knowing that they have the capacity to help others.

One such group is currently being formed. Only a few students will have this opportunity at a time. Your child has shown an interest in participating in the organization, which will begin following this vacation. We will meet twice a week during Team Time on Tuesdays and Fridays.

If you agree to allow your child to participate, please fill out the attached permission slip and send it back to my attention by Friday, 2/18 or the first day of school following vacation. If you have any questions, please call me at my home or here at school.

V. Sgambato

———

At one point in my career, the sessions took place during Team Time, a period during which the students could seek extra help in a particular subject, use the time for a study hall, volunteer to help other students or a particular teacher, or attend special lessons arranged by several teachers and the administration. During another part of my career, we met immediately following lunch. There were times when I also arranged to facilitate a meeting at the end of the day; transportation arrangements, of course, had to be made.

THE FOLLOWING EVALUATIONS WERE PASSED OUT AT THE END OF EVERY SEMESTER:

A number of responses are included; they were chosen at random from many received and not altered in any way. All replies were made while group members were in the sixth grade.

What, in your opinion, is the purpose of our sessions held twice a week?

- To help people feel good about themselves.

- To let our feelings out and to seek answers to our problems.

- To be able to discuss your problems with friends and to help other people with their problems.

- To help and be helped.

- To let children deal with their feelings.

- To help people if they have problems.

- The group's purpose of meeting is so children can express feelings.

Have our sessions been of help to you? _____ If so, how?

- Yes, because we are all nice people.

- Definitely! It gives me an outlet for my feelings, and it lets me help others. It makes me feel good to know I can help the other kids.

- Yes, because I've been able to help other people with their problems.

- Yes. I like helping people and having someone to talk to.

- Yes. I can express myself in a way I never do.

- To say what I have kept inside all this time.

- Yes, because the group helped me get closer to my father.

What did you like least about them?
- Nothing.

- That we only had them twice a week, and <u>then</u>, they had to stop completely!!! (end of year)

- The end…and people have sad problems.

- Time!

- Not lots of time.

- I like everything.

- Nothing.

Are there any suggestions that you could make to improve future group sessions?
- No, not that I could think of

- Have more of them!

- No, the sessions are good as they are.

- ?

- No

- That we should get more people in here to tell if they have any problems.

- I have no suggestions. The group is great. I just wish we could meet for a longer period of time.

General comments:
- I like the group very much.

- Rap On!

- I like this group and I wish there was more time.

- Hopefully, I helped.

- It was fun. I hope for years that will follow (others) will enjoy the experience.

- It was great coming.

- My father and I are now much closer.

-Additional responses not quoted here appear to be very close in nature to the replies above.

HOW TO BEGIN

Members need to feel welcome and comfortable before beginning to share their private concerns and feelings. This, I believe, would be the first of the facilitator's objectives. Do not expect that individuals will immediately begin divulging private, personal information about themselves. It may take a bit of time.

However, when I became better versed, so to speak, in the art of "welcoming and relaxing" the members of the groups, there were occasions when they came ready to speak, and actually did so.

In addition to any preparatory strategies you may assemble through your own means, here are a few suggestions I'll make based upon my experience:

- Ease the members into the group setting in a warm and friendly manner. Then, after making sure everyone is acquainted, ask them to describe what they believe is the group's purpose.

- Clear up any misconceptions immediately.

- Stress the importance of confidentiality and respect.

- Ask everyone: "Why did you agree to join?"

- Be patient with members; it may take a bit of time before they begin divulging their problems.

- Additionally, instruct all members to be patient rather than to interrupt their classmates; it is not a casual conversation.

- Request that the speaker let everyone know when he or she has concluded—for example, by saying, "I'm done." It is not always apparent to all that the individual has completed describing the problem and is waiting for responses.

- At times, a group member may forget to announce that he or she is done describing a difficulty. Therefore, after an appropriate amount of time, someone may simply ask, "Are you done, Mary?"

- If you perceive, however, that the individual has concluded, it would be appropriate for you to comment: "Nicely done, Mary. If anyone wishes to respond to Mary's concerns, now would be the time." Or you could make comments, perhaps leading her in thought. Nudge her a bit in a "helpful direction." Or, if it's time to wind up: "Mary, are you comfortable in putting some of the suggestions to work for yourself?" "Perhaps think about your current experience and let us know in our next session as to your decisions or how you've progressed."

- Remind all members to wait for an appropriate amount of time before checking with the speaker as to completion.

- Once having begun, get other members involved: "What is your reaction to Mary's problem, Sam?" "Has anyone else had a similar experience?"

- Don't move in quickly to "save the day." "Quick-fix" remedies may give the student the impression that you think he or she is "not smart enough" to figure it out alone. Toss in questions, possibly guiding the speaker in a direction to a solution. Look around, perceiving members' expressions. Then, perhaps, ask one of them for a comment.

- Give group members, rather than the facilitator, the first opportunity to suggest possible directions to embark upon.

- Don't take the floor away by stating that you totally understand the difficulty and easily propose a solution. "Same thing happened to me when I was your age. Here's what I did..."

- Preach **patience** whenever possible. Repeat from time to time that they may have to put their concerns on hold for a time...maybe, even until the next session.

- If tears are shed, absolutely do not say anything like, "It's OK, Jeanie, it's OK." If all were OK, she would not be crying.

Sadness and tears are part of living just as are laughter and joy. Allow Jeanie to express her feelings openly. (And always have tissues available for Jeanie and anyone else emotionally moved by her tears.)

- Avoid making judgments: "You're taking this too seriously." "I'd just stop talking to that person if I were you." This does *not* help.

- Do not minimize the problem: "I'm sure you'll feel differently about this in a week or so." Again, it is not the solution to the existing problem for the kid.

- As you near the end of the year, with few sessions remaining, you might have a short discussion. Remind them how many gatherings are left. Possibly pursue the question, "What will you do about any personal concerns once the group no longer meets?" "How will you deal with any problems?" "Whom will you talk to about difficulties?" ...and, let them know how you feel about the sessions and the bonds: "I will miss seeing you and talking to you after the year ends...but I won't forget you."

At typical group sessions, we discussed difficulties occurring between students, among family members, and between students and teachers. Many of the concerns were typical for early adolescents. Although I strongly suspected that some of the concerns would be discarded in a short time, if it was important to the student on a particular day, it, consequently, became imperative for the group to focus upon the concern and offer support. On occasions, we heard of difficulties relating to the loss of family members and pets, misunderstandings between friends, the emotional confusion regarding parental discipline, and much more.

From time to time, I did enlist the assistance of certain colleagues and professionals as indicated earlier. However, suggestions offered by members of the group frequently made very good sense to the recipients as well as to myself—sometimes, surprisingly so.

———

The Support Group is not *the* answer to all adolescent difficulties. I believe, however, that it does provide *an* answer; *one* piece of the puzzle. Will it turn the life of a potential bully or brooding, depressed teen around 180 degrees? Possibly.... But even if not, it may get his or her attention for a period of time. And during that interval, we have the opportunity to apply a thought-out, strategic means of intervention (clinical or otherwise) which may very well motivate the individual to:

- Reconsider his or her thoughts, recognize his or her peer support, and, additionally, one's potential.

- Reconsider the value and abilities of his or her peers.

- ....And,...most importantly, reduce or even avoid the options of anger or violence.

———

TESTIMONY FROM FORMER MEMBERS

Below are comments recently made by three former group members. The individuals are today in their mid-twenties. The responses sum up what they recall from their Support Group experiences:

David Kellett, presently a fifth-grade teacher:

Looking back to my sixth-grade experiences as a member of Mr. Sgambato's organized group, there are several memories that stick in my mind.

One of which is trustworthiness, both by Mr. Sgambato and the other group members. The group consisted of several students from differing backgrounds, abilities and interests. Although I will openly admit my past hesitance to even join the group because of this and my speculation that other students had the same apprehension (because most sixth graders would normally prefer a group to be filled solely with their best of friends), Mr. Sgambato established a safe and secure environment that made all members feel comfortable. Right from the first meeting, we knew that whatever was spoken in the group was confidential. We knew that we had a responsibility to respect each other's thoughts and feelings. No matter everyone's background, we were at the same level here. We could communicate openly, without fear of peer judgment.

I also remember the group's sincerity. Because of the environment that was developed by the facilitator, we felt comfortable being active participants. Kids were honest and open with each other, and Mr. Sgambato was always the same with us. Speakers sometimes wore their hearts on their sleeves, as did some listeners. I still recall specific accounts from sixth grade because of the emotions attached. We all resonated with each other's stories in some way, and we bonded together as the sessions continued.

Most of all, I remember the kinship. We were united by each other's personal stories and words of encouragement. I remember moments of sadness and moments of uplifting, and I always felt accepted.

Looking back at my experience from the scope of a teacher, I am even more impressed with the positivity a group such as this presents. It builds on an individual's confidence, maturity, trust, and respect. Additionally, it has a positive effect on communication and social skills, both with peers and adults. I strongly recommend a program such as Mr. Sgambato's for any school.

David Kellett
5th Grade Teacher
Maryland City Elementary School

Jan Williams, presently a stay-at-home mother
I'm a 26 years old, stay at home mother of two beautiful children, and still working as a photographer here and there.
Hello Mr. Sgambato,

The group to me was a way for each one of us to listen to each other and hear how related our lives were. Remembering it helped me realize that at that time in my life, everyone had problems and it felt really nice to have someone listen or even someone to talk to.

I think it's great that you are going to try to get the schools involved into these support groups. Kids of all ages need to know that they can talk to someone and learn different ways of dealing with their feelings no matter what the issue may be. Best of luck with book and project.

Jan

Cory White:

In his mid-twenties, a new dad, and graduate of Fort Plain Central School, class of 2006:

In 2000, when I was in the 6th grade, my English teacher, Mr. Sgambato, approached a group of ten or so students about the formation of a "Support Group." We were to talk about anything…from homework to girls and boys, parents, "growing pains," or more personal things. And the best part was we were able to speak freely. Many of us didn't want to talk to our parents all the time. I struggled with problems, but wouldn't talk to mine. I relied upon the group. It helped me with many difficulties.

In this day, I feel that these "Support Groups" would benefit many students…just to have a place to talk things out. Many kids don't get the chance to talk things out until it's too late. Too often some are resorting to physical violence to solve their problems. I believe with more groups like this, we all could help put an end to events such as Newtown or suicides. Simply listen to what the kids are trying to tell you. Everyone wants to give opinions as to what you or I should or shouldn't do, but are not willing to listen to what the kids would tell them. Cory

CHAPTER 12: MULTICULTURAL EDUCATION

I understand why America is often referred to as a **"melting pot."** I believe, however, that a more accurate, realistic term describing our country would be a **"stew."** All citizens do not live a *mixture* of similar lives; they are each *different* from one another. And that's *fine!* This analogy is one I borrowed from the A World of Difference Campaign (its primary objective: Reducing prejudice). It was sponsored by The Anti-Defamation League of B'nai B'rith under the direction of Neal and Jane Golub. I worked as a trainer for several years.

Ethnicity, religion, skin color, language, culture.... These "differences," exist within our nation...with each being a chunk, a part of America. The question is...have the majority of our people truly become accepting, understanding, tolerant, and, less prejudiced? I do believe there is a positive movement underway; the country is, indeed, progressing in the right direction. A helpful strategy would be for our teachers to enhance the transition by developing programs giving our younger generation opportunities to move even closer together in learning, understanding, accepting, and... *celebrating* different cultural traditions.

In this way, our citizens can be encouraged to **share the diversities**. Americans can live their lives taking part in each other's ethnic diversities and celebrations rather than existing in separate cultures isolated from one another. Consequently, the movement toward a society where everyone is truly understood and accepted will be more quickly achieved.

Our teachers can do much to enhance multicultural acceptance while they counter the existence of bigotry in our nation...not by lecturing, however. It changes little in student attitudes toward different cultures. Becoming personally involved in Multicultural Education, on the other hand, provides our kids with experiences directed toward accepting dissimilarities as well as the skills necessary in recognizing and rejecting prejudiced behaviors. Too many regard the unfamiliar with suspicion and aversion. Logical strategies to employ, therefore, would be to:

- Acquaint our kids with cultures that may appear unfamiliar to them.

- Allow our young people to see evidence that ethnic groups from many parts of the world have made significant contributions to the American experience.

- View these multicultural achievements taking place in America as evidence that we share a kinship with one another.

Each minority has the right, of course, to enjoy its heritage. Members experience greater pride, identity, and resilience when their own roots are explored and appreciated. Additionally, when a majority of our American population succeeds in co-mingling and sharing dialogue based upon ethnicity, more meaningful progress is achieved.

By introducing an actual *multicultural curriculum* with enlightening classroom activities, teachers can promote the idea that diversity is a strength of our nation, not a liability. This principle would help to nurture the harmony necessary for a brighter, more prosperous future for generations. Opposing arguments foster anger, disenchantment, and failure on the part of our culture.

A reduction in prejudiced thoughts and behaviors is more likely experienced by students when appropriate classroom activities are used that require them to become <u>personally</u> involved in the lesson. Teachers can approach this topic by reading and discussing books and other forms of literature based upon topics such as:

- The Holocaust

- Apartheid

- Racism

- Tolerance

- The American Japanese Evacuation during WWII

- The Montgomery County Bus Boycott

- The lives of Martin Luther King, Rosa Parks, as well as a number of other related topics or similar themes.

Students may read silently or orally, discussing the topics at length. This helps them develop a greater appreciation for America's cultural differences and also become aware as to what some members of ethnic groups have had to deal with. The class, as a whole, will come to understand that we are not a homogeneous society. We are different. And these dissimilarities should be viewed as complementary. We need to reach out to one another and share our differences, to celebrate them, to enjoy them.

The theme of avoiding prejudice can be pursued in reading, writing, and discussions held within class community meetings. The teacher can also include a list of spelling words based upon the theme as well—("prejudice," "stereotyping," "tolerance," "scapegoating," bigotry,...). In addition to holding participants responsible for their correct spelling, they can be quizzed on the definitions, as well, being able to properly use the words in sentences. This tactic strongly enhances the important themes of tolerance and compassion while emphasizing the uselessness of discrimination.

Following class discussions, writing assignments could thereafter be promoted dealing with the unit topics. Suggestions could be sought as to how individuals may confront the problems. (Example: What would it be like if you were treated differently because of a physical characteristic over which you had absolutely no control?) Compositions could be shared and discussed with classmates.

Additionally, speakers might be brought in who might address a variety of topics dealing with prejudiced behavior as it affects victims _and_ perpetrators. Presentations could be based upon diversity, racism, physically challenged individuals, boycotting, scapegoating, stereotyping, ethnic jokes, and gay-bashing.

While in the classroom, we viewed a number of videos describing true accounts of discrimination in America along with the difficulties experienced by citizens who, in the minds of some, were regarded as, **"different, unacceptable, and unequal."** Experiences like these truly brought the dilemma into the lives of my students...but nothing was as powerful the following "experiment" that I initiated in dealing with the topic.

For several years, I conducted the following activity in my classroom, providing my kids with a unique and quite personal encounter based upon the stigmas of bigotry and intolerance. Though it was difficult to administer, it taught a valuable lesson. The "Blue Eyes—Brown Eyes Experiment" was originally pioneered by an Iowa elementary teacher named Jane Elliot who allowed her third-grade class to experience a first-hand reaction to discrimination.

The following experience powerfully influenced most of my students over a period of several years. Today, they still remember. Read the comments contributed by former class members, now adults, at the end of the chapter.

Prejudice must be addressed....

STANDING IN SOMEONE ELSE'S SHOES

She was easily one of the most gifted composers in my sixth-grade writing class...a likable, well-behaved, talented eleven-year-old student. And there she sat tearing her homework into shreds and throwing it on the floor. Behind the tears in her eyes, a glare of defiance was unmistakable.

It had not been particularly difficult obtaining that reaction from her. Nor was I surprised when observing evidence of frustration and anger surfacing in other members of my class. I'd opened my writing lesson with a statement: "We're going to conduct an experiment." With that, I divided my class into two groups; one section made up of brown-eyed students and the other composed of blue-eyed kids.

Having already decided to award privileges to the brown-eyed bunch, I invited them to relax on the rug in the middle of the room and peruse magazines. I encouraged them to read, laugh, and enjoy the publications while complimenting them on their choices and willingness to share their thoughts with other brown-eyed students.

The blue-eyed students, on the other hand, were told to remain in their seats and complete a tedious and boring grammar assignment. My manner with them was rigid, perhaps even unfriendly. Through a series of prejudiced remarks, I made it apparent to all that I didn't expect much success from the group seated at its desks. Citing a non-existent theory I referred to as "Brown-Eyed Supremacy," I let it be known that the blue-eyed crowd couldn't possibly measure up. Having blue eyes, they simply lacked the potential. I almost rudely kept them on task, while commenting a time or two about their blue-eyed appearance and its responsibility for their inferiority.

It was only a matter of minutes before the environment of the room became totally influenced by what I had instigated. My discriminating remarks aimed at the blue-eyed members soon inspired similar insensitive comments from the privileged students. The relationships among class members began to deteriorate rapidly as a polarization brought about bickering, sadness, anger, and even tears.

Despite our earlier class discussions centered around prejudice, discrimination, and stereotyping, these children were easily motivated to exhibit types of behavior that they had earlier identified as unfair and ugly. Their conduct, in fact, was such that I momentarily found myself experiencing reservations over its need of completion despite what I anticipated was an important lesson.

Though the egregious splintering among my students continued, I stood firm, reasoning that completing the unorthodox experiment might, in fact, serve to <u>intensify</u> the lesson's significance for the entire class. It would more easily help us understand how quickly we can be led to discrimination simply because of the ease with which we may follow an example set by others. And so, the lesson continued....

The two groups, more than likely, assumed that leaving my room that day meant leaving the experiment behind. Unknown to them, I had enlisted the help of a number of my colleagues who agreed to subtly remind the kids, throughout the day, of the physical difference that existed between them. For example, the brown-eyed group might be allowed to leave a class first, or get drinks, or choose gym equipment before the blue-eyed students...anything to reinforce the notion that inferiority and discrimination existed.

On the second day, I **reversed** the process, making the members of the brown-eyed group the objects of scorn and slurs. Though I began to experience some difficulty looking into the eyes of my kids, I again concluded that the results would be ultimately worth the discomfort. My plan was to allow each group nearly a full day of "mistreatment" before finally bringing the lesson to a close.

The third day arrived; it was finally over. The class sat on the rug for a debriefing session. The first thing I needed to do was to profoundly apologize to all...I did so. I then attempted to justify the experience while at the same time describing my genuine uneasiness with what had transpired. We discussed the activity at length. Though we knew it was an experiment, its intensity was still surprisingly strong and effective. For the remainder of the period, we discussed the following questions:

- What evidence was there of my treating people differently?

- Did individuals feel angry at the other group? Why?

- Did anyone feel angry at the teacher?

- Did any changes take place in the way people treated each other outside of the classroom?

- How does everyone feel about that now?

- Even though no one in the class is inferior, did anyone begin to feel as though he or she really was as a result of the activity?

- The discrimination was based upon a variance in eye color; a physical difference over which participants had absolutely no control. How do you feel about that? Can the experiment be compared to situations that exist in the real world?

Near the end of the discussion, one girl pointed out the following: Though she understood the purpose of the lesson, she felt that, by involving other teachers throughout the day, I had overstepped the requirements of the experiment. Several others echoed the sentiment that I might have gone further than necessary. I asked for a raising of hands on the part of those that felt I'd gone too far. Nearly every hand was raised. After a short pause, I replied slowly and quietly, "You had to put up with this nonsense for forty-eight hours. There are people in this world, in this country, in this very community, who put up with it *every day of their lives.*"

Every head then turned in my direction. It was as though I had unwittingly provided the final piece to some complex puzzle. All eyes seemed to reflect a sudden and sad awareness of the lesson's most significant purpose. If a climax to the experiment existed, we reached it at that moment. Not until that point had any individual successfully applied the learning experience to real life.

We spent the next few lessons taking a close look at the absurdity of stereotypical generalizations by reading and discussing several true accounts of Americans forced to suffer humiliation, disrespect, and even injury and death, all caused by blatant ignorance and prejudice on the part of their fellow countrymen.

Their comments and behavior took on a sincerity and passion I'd rarely observed in my students prior to that day. It became clear that they felt a desire...a need...to explore what prejudice is really all about. This was not difficult to understand. What was surprising was the direction the project took at this point.

My class decided, without my help, to develop a workshop encouraging participants to check their attitudes regarding prejudice and discrimination. They didn't, as I expected, however, wish to invite another group of students to take part in the workshop...they wanted to target their parents! As the idea took shape, I suggested that it might be better to deal with people of the same age. They unanimously held to their original idea. I'd never experienced such determination. I relinquished. Each class member took home an invitation asking mothers and fathers to attend a function sponsored by the entire class. However, no parent was informed as to the purpose of the affair. (This was the kids' idea.)

Upon entering my classroom a week later, parents were immediately exposed to a blue eyes/brown eyes role-play. Following this introductory scenario, they viewed a video segment of discrimination in action. In all, there were sixteen pieces to the two-hour program. Included were definitions and discussions surrounding key words such as "scapegoating" and "prejudice," original compositions describing our blue eyes/brown eyes ordeal, accounts of how the experiment affected a number of students, several video vignettes developed by the "A World of Difference" project, a few activities designed to motivate discussion over what discrimination is and isn't, and actual accounts of individuals experiencing prejudice in our society. And who was in charge of the workshop? Who directed the flow of its components that evening? The teacher, right? Wrong...

Each part of the evening was guided by one of my students. I was a member of the audience. I'd given them two class periods to develop their own approaches. Consequently, from beginning to end, the adults were led by their children through a workshop agenda designed to motivate discussion as well as sincere soul-searching. During the encounter, our guests raised a number of questions and concerns. Some of the comments made were:

"I'm Scottish, and occasionally, friends tell Scottish jokes. I'm not offended."

"My husband is Polish and I'm Italian. We sometimes jokingly use names with each other that you might label as derogatory. Does this mean that we're discriminating?"

"If we can't tell ethnic jokes, there aren't a whole lot of jokes left that we can tell, are there?"

Though I was able to express myself freely on several occasions, more frequently, I relinquished the floor to a determined sixth-grader requesting, "Can I answer that?"…or…"I wanna say something, Mr. Sgambato."

More often than not, I sat back and joined the rest of the audience in listening to the young people's arguments. Ethnic jokes may not offend some, but others within earshot might be offended. Are adults setting good examples for their children? Who benefits from bigoted slurs? One boy pointed out that ethnic jokes could prove to be an embarrassing habit. "Ethnic jokes could increase feelings of prejudice in others," commented another determined young lady. As I looked around the room, it appeared that several adults were still somewhat amused at the prospect of being guided through a workshop by their children. At the same time, however, there was no question that the students' statements were, at the very least, inspiring most of the adults to ponder the meaning of it all.

The honesty and determination expressed by my students on the evening frankly surprised and impressed me. I was pleased and extremely proud of them. On the following day, we recounted our experience and its effects upon all concerned. The event seemed to deepen the children's commitment to being fair towards others. I believe that the evening nurtured a better understanding of inequality and a determination to do something about it. For the remainder of the year, and years to follow, students continued to comment on the direction and progress of our common cause.

Did we persuade a room full of parents not to ever tell or laugh at an ethnic joke? Probably not. I do feel, however, that we did succeed in getting at least some of those folks to take a second look at their own feelings, to consider their own ethics, their own senses of dignity and fairness. I offer this note from a mother as evidence:

Dear Mr. Sgambato and students,

"Thank you for inviting your parents to your presentation, 'A World of Difference.' Through sharing what you have recently experienced, you have given me a greater insight on discrimination. Your knowledge and sensitivity of the subject made the evening a memorable one. Keep up the good work."

As for the youngsters I chose to expose to this rather risky lesson, will their passion for fairness survive their entry into adulthood,...or even junior high school? I'd be indulging a rather lofty fantasy if I stated that the values highlighted by our experiment would be certain to last a lifetime. Their views would, in all probability, be tempered by time, experience, and peer influence. But, I feel quite confident in believing that the time they spent in the shoes of another human being did, during their sixth grade year, at any rate, make A World of Difference. They will, at the very least, _remember_.

Please read on....

———

The above piece was written a number of years ago. At the end of it, I admitted doubt that the experience would "last a lifetime." Could I have been wrong?

As I indicated earlier, it is always a pleasure when encountering former students. We chat, chuckle, and reminisce. I recently caught up with two gentlemen who were members of a class during the time that the event described above took place.

Joseph Kardash is now in his mid-thirties and enjoys the position of school superintendent in the Colton Pierrepont School System located in the Adirondack Mountains of upstate New York. He was kind enough to respond to a couple of questions I proposed. They follow:

1. What do you recall of the event?

"I remember being offended when the experiment continued outside the classroom. I didn't like having my day messed with outside of class. The strongest memory is voicing my distaste for disrupting my day only to be asked the question, 'How do you think people feel that have to deal with this every day?' The feeling of that moment is burned in the memory of many of my classmates."

2. Did it affect you?...and if so, how?

"I was fortunate to realize the importance of understanding other people's perspective at the early age of twelve. This skill has grown beyond recognition of discrimination into one of my strengths. It helps in every aspect of dealing with people and situations, thanks to an early start in Mr. Sgambato's sixth grade class."

Joe Kardash
Superintendent
Colton Pierrepont School System
New York

Jacob Darrow, also in his thirties, is a third and fourth grade teacher who truly enjoys his students. I asked Jacob the same questions as I asked Joe Kardash. His response follows:

"I remember your lesson on discrimination like it happened yesterday. I remember every detail from it. I recall the students with blue eyes getting to eat Doritos and the chilling tone in your voice as you spoke to the students with brown eyes. It was the most powerful lesson I ever experienced in a class. At the time, being in sixth grade, I never really thought about what discrimination was. All I knew was that I got chips and you were being extra nice to me. I also remember knowing there was something wrong with how you were treating the students with brown eyes.

I remember seeing the faces of the other students, the sadness in their eyes, and it made me sad. Your lesson taught me a valuable lesson, one that I teach my own children and students. I teach them to treat everyone with kindness and respect. Everyone is different and deserves to be respected. I still make reference to your lesson with my own third and fourth grade students. Vic, you are one of the reasons I wanted to become a teacher and make a real difference in the lives of my students as you did in mine so many years ago."

Jacob Darrow

Yes, though you may be unaware of each occurrence, you touch their lives,…and their futures…. You… influence your students…. Think about it.

THE LAST CHAPTER

As the day of my retirement grew near, my thoughts about the move increased dramatically.

Questions began to form in my mind:

- How was I to respond when asked, "What do you do?" {I *was* a teacher; I *am* a teacher; I am a *retired* teacher}

- How will I feel on a daily basis? Won't the absence of my educational responsibilities and a classroom full of kids leave a void in my existence? How do I fill it?

- When a conversation is taking place near me, and I overhear a "teacher term" resonating in the dialogue ("faculty meeting, third quarter average, curriculum, IEP"), will I feel left out...as though I'd still like to be involved in the conversation?

- Will I feel disconnected, no longer a part of "the group"?

- That "special place" will cease to exist...no classroom. No place to take interesting facts, motivating strategies, new ideas, funny events. Where do I go to get the feel of early adolescence? How will I deal with its loss?

The following question may occur to the reader: If I enjoyed teaching so much, why did I leave the profession? It boils down to money. The story goes like this: There existed a financial incentive to retire. You know, one of those "backward things." (Let's give our most experienced teachers a chunk of cash to leave; then *we'll* save money) Additionally, the agreement, at that time, stated that we would only be responsible for paying only 5 percent of our health insurance for the rest of our lives. The teachers' union was scheduled to negotiate once again with the board of education the following year. No one with whom I spoke felt that both the incentive and the reduced health insurance payment would still be part of the new contract. Hence, it was time to depart. I didn't like it, but felt it would better serve my future interest.

———

LAST DAY

It indeed arrived…my Last Day as a teacher. I told myself to stay focused on my responsibilities and not let my mind wander into emotional arenas. I would "get the job done," then wander off to relax and enjoy. As you might expect, the encounter was considerably more difficult. At the very end of the day, we exchanged our sad good-byes as my students slowly filed out of the room; I sat at my desk for the last time and began writing a description of my last movements, thoughts, and emotions while in my classroom for the final time. They appear below:

MY WRITTEN THOUGHTS FROM THE DAY:
June 22, 2000 / 1:20 P.M.:

"Kids yelling, bodies moving, large cardboard boxes in rooms being filled with bright-colored trash,…noise…teachers buzzing, people walking, rapid movements, anxiety, stress. It's June 22, 2000. It's hot. It's loud. It's my last day as a professional teacher….

My room looks so different, almost alien in appearance. All my personal possessions, **gone**. Walls bare; empty. As I enter, I pause for a moment, allowing my eyes to pass over the desks and chairs that have been my hub of activity for thirty-five years.

I stand alone in the empty room, slowly turning around,...and around.... Time has gone by. It's now become so strangely quiet. The deafening silence seems quite appropriate, offering evidence of the end of a chapter; the end of a career. I feel as though my lungs can't pull in enough oxygen to sustain a satisfactory breath. As I make my way across the floor, my body seems to experience resistance, as though a density resides, impairing my movement through the room. My existence in this environment seems suddenly surreal. Am I really here?

Two-twenty-five...if today were a full day of school, the kids would be getting out in thirteen minutes.

A colleague stops in...notices my moist eyes...then assures me, *"We'll still be here, Vic."* (Yes, but I won't.) She then turns and hurries down the hall.

There appears to be an amber tint to the room...as though representing a scene from my past...what used to be, rather than what *is*. Time, however, appears irrelevant; this could be any year...1998, 1977, 1966...I'm so cramped...can't breathe. The amber doesn't go away...the color surrounds me. This is nuts...surreal....

The silence is overwhelming...only the hum of the fans, the sound of my fingers hitting the keyboard, a distant conversation miles down the corridor. I look up...and quietly stare.

The amber tint has increased; is this real? I ask myself again,...am I really here? From where have these young faces suddenly come...staring at me, waiting for me to start my lesson. Why are they here? *"Please begin, Mr. Sgambato."* They are so impatient. They're waiting, but seem anxious, friendly...some with just a hint of a smile (we've shared so many giggles and chuckles) *"Why aren't you teaching, Mr. Sgambato?"* Chad is seated in the front seat of the middle row; I haven't seen him in years. They continue to wait; I cannot speak...I simply stare....

It's over? Truly, it has passed...it's gone...forever. I'm done. Why is it so damn hard to breathe?

The faces dissolve, disappear. They knew they weren't supposed to be here. It's my time to be alone....

Two-twenty-three; if this were a full day of school, the kids would be leaving in five minutes. There would be five minutes left to the day...five minutes. I just can't seem to catch a breath!

It's so difficult to conclude this lesson...yet, I have no choice; I must end it. I need to leave. **It's over.**" (6/22/00...2:26 P.M.)

———

For those of you in "mid-stream" or perhaps nearing the last few years of your careers, do you remember

• Your first interview?

• The first time you entered your classroom?

• Your first class? (How old are they now?)

• The first time you wrote your name on the board? (Did it look strange? How did it feel? What were you thinking?)

• How many students have you taught?

• With how many colleagues have you shared your career? (Where are they now?)

Why did you enter the teaching profession? Was it to make a difference in the lives of your students?

As my last school year moved toward its completion, I knew that my time in attempting to make a difference was limited. I endeavored, therefore, to be even *more* tolerant, *more* patient, take *more* time with the difficult kids...touch more, especially the ones who needed to be touched.

Then my career became sharply limited. I had only days left to make a difference. And finally...it drew to a close.

Your time to affect your students' lives continues to exist. However, it too, is <u>limited</u> and lives within a timeframe. Make the most of it...every day. Good luck to you...and to all your students.

———

APPENDIX:

LESSON PLAN COMPONENTS

LESSON TITLE

<u>Objectives</u>: Expected learner outcomes. Purpose(s), goal(s) of the lesson.

<u>Anticipatory Set</u>: Specific activities or statements used to motivate students, to focus them upon the lesson. This opening connects the students to the upcoming lesson.

<u>Input</u>: Information provided that is essential for the students to know before beginning the lesson. This segment also explains how the information will be communicated to them.

<u>Instruction</u>: Procedure and content of lesson. Presentation of concepts and lesson information.

<u>Guided Practice</u>: While supervised, students are led through activities which give them the opportunity to practice and apply the skills and/or information provided to them.

<u>Closure</u>: How the lesson will be "wrapped up." This is where the lesson is reviewed and the purpose is given meaning.

<u>Independent Practice</u>: Homework or seatwork assigned to ensure that they've mastered the skills, along with understanding the lesson's purpose and goals.

LESSON PLANS

LESSON 1. RECIPE FOR HOMEWORK SUCCESS (P. 82 IN TEXT)

Objectives:

1. To allow pupils to freely discuss and even vent difficulties incurred while addressing homework assignments.

2. To encourage class members to consider reasons *why* homework is given.

3. To engage students in an active session within which they discuss and share potentially worthwhile approaches in successfully completing homework assignments.

4. To develop a list of homework strategies for all to consider using in the future.

Anticipatory Set

1. Initiate a discussion based upon homework, encouraging positive as well as negative comments. (Possibly begin by offering an earlier experience with a challenging homework assignment from your own past or from a former student's encounter)

2. Be clear that any honest response is welcome. Responses offered by students may be written on newsprint, Smartboard, etc. by the teacher.

Instruction:

1. Divide students into groups of two, directing them to focus upon complaints expressed by classmates earlier in the lesson and discuss ways of addressing the concerns in a positive fashion. (If they wish, students may take notes.)

2. After bringing the group back together in a Community Meeting, ask that they brainstorm solutions one concern at a time, as you write them clearly on Smartboard, newsprint, etc.

3. Edit the brainstormed list of suggestions until the students are satisfied that the list poses strong, usable strategies for dealing with the homework concerns.

4. Display the list clearly in the classroom. At a later time, present each student with individual copies to use when faced with similar concerns.

CHECK FOR UNDERSTANDING:

1. Refer to the list of suggestions in the future whenever appropriate.

2. Ask class to reflect upon and share any strategies they identified as helpful in successfully completing complicated assignments.

The following is a list of those suggestions mentioned most often in my classes:

1. Don't forget to use your assignment pad, iPod, iPad, Smartphone, etc. to *keep track of assignments.*

2. Be sure that you *understand the directions* before leaving school.

3. Make good use of *study halls.*

4. *Organize your materials* in your binder and in your locker.

5. Do your work at the same time daily. *Follow a schedule.*

6. Find a quiet, comfortable *place to work*...away from the TV.

7. *Don't procrastinate.*

8. Take a *break* if you have a lot to do.

9. Put completed homework in a place where you *won't lose or forget it.*

10. Have someone in mind to contact when needing homework *advice.*

(Refer to the list as necessary...or add to it)
Kindly keep my earlier description of Ronald in mind (the boy whose home I visited. Homework assumes that there is a "Home.")

Closure: At the conclusion of the original session, ask each class member to write down and suggestions on the list from which they may benefit.

LESSON 2. THE MILLING ASSASSIN (P. 94 IN TEXT):

(Listed as Activity #1 in text) Functions as a "first step" in the process of peer acceptance and bonding, encouraging a Team Approach to classroom challenges. Though it may sound rather strange at first, it has practical benefits. I used it yearly. It works. Try it.

Objectives:

1. To encourage interaction, enhance trust, reduce discomfort, and energize class members.

2. To break through potentially existing barriers among students.

3. To begin a lesson, session, week, or semester in an active, unorthodox, positive manner.

Anticipatory Set:

1. Introduce the following: Two strategies that help in dealing with personal problems, discomfort, disappointment (The two strategies suggested below are helpful in "setting the stage,"...getting them

in an appropriate frame of mind. However, with time restraints, one or both can be eliminated if necessary).

a. **Support network**: Friends and family members available to be approached with personal concerns. "When you are experiencing any kind of difficulties,...school problems, personal problems, health concerns,...anything...and feel a need for support and advice, what steps can you take?" (Seek trusted friends and family.) This is essential for everyone. We all need support at times in our lives.

- Without disclosing names of friends or family, each student is encouraged to have one or more individuals in mind during the lesson.

- Briefly discuss examples of support experienced by teacher and class members along with the advantages of utilizing the support.

b. **An active sense of humor**: Humor can help "reframe" potentially depressing situations, promote the release of endorphins, and build resilience within the individual. A well-functioning sense of humor helps one see difficult situations in a different, more realistic light.

- Offer amusing occurrences from your life that helped you deal with challenging times. Ask for humorous examples from the class. Brief discussion.

- Then, taking advantage of their amused frames of mind, move immediately from the existing humorous environment into the activity described below:

Instruction:
1. Introduce "The Milling Assassin," explaining rules and procedure beforehand.

2. Move around the outside of a circle of students standing with their eyes closed and hands open behind them.
3. Pull on the index finger of each, except for the student you've secretly chosen to portray the Milling Assassin. Instead, touch the middle of the palm.
4. Announce: "Go ahead and mill." Students wander about silently, shaking hands (and smiling like crazy...they can't help it).
5. When "The Assassin" feels he/she can get away with it, while shaking hands, the index finger is extended to touch the wrist area of the unsuspecting classmate.
6. After receiving the "Death Tap," the victim silently counts to 10, then falls to the floor, making any appropriate vocal noises he/she wishes. No one else may speak. Counting to 10 allows the "assassin" to move away from the victim and not be easily identified.
7. If a student feels he/she knows who the Assassin is, he/she may raise a hand and ask the facilitator to stop the action. The facilitator then asks the class for a second individual to raise a hand in order to "back up" the guess to be made by the first individual. (you need two participants involved in order to officially offer a guess as to identifying the Assassin.) After someone volunteers to "back up" the first student, he/she is then given the opportunity to identify the Assassin. If the individuals are correct, the Assassin has been successfully identified and the first session concludes.
8. If the individuals are incorrect, both also "die" and fall to the floor. Continue milling.

Closure: Through "processing" the activity:
This offers a "look back," a manner of reviewing an activity in such a way that the participants better understand its purpose. They may also

examine what they were thinking, feeling, and doing during the flow. They may then more easily perceive the benefits of engaging the lesson and what can be learned from it (about each other and about working together).

Processing could include the use of helpful questions such as:

- "Why do you think I introduced the lesson?"

- "What did you learn about yourself, classmates, your teacher, school…?"

- "What surprised you?"

- "What would you change in the activity to make the lesson more interesting?"

- "How are you feeling about what we just did?"

Are they in a lighter mood? Might they be viewing classmates a bit differently?

Have connections and relationships among them been improved?

The processing component may include the teacher simply feeding back to the kids what he or she had observed—speed with which work was done, conversations engaged, who got out of the chair first, who approached a classmate quickly or slowly, first or last, who smiled, etc., in order to allow the class an opportunity to review the activity and understand participants' different interpretations of the task.

Example:

"I observed several rise from their chairs rather quickly and begin forming a circle when told to do so. The majority of the class, however, rose more slowly, heads turning to look around the room, and did not seem to be in a hurry. Once the exercise was underway, there were smiles and laughter. This appears rather normal for a group this size. I've seen the same reaction with high school seniors, teachers, and even parents when engaged in this activity. Now, I could be wrong, but some seemed...well...a bit reluctant at first, to get moving, but then eventually joined in. I loved every moment!"

———

The practice of **processing** helps everyone understand how the class is doing and validates the reality that some class members have different perceptions and reactions to the task. They may come to recognize that their classmates view the lesson a bit differently, and it may even give them a new perspective on the activity as well as on their peers.

Additionally, some may respond to future classroom encounters with greater enthusiasm and optimism, and less hesitancy.

Repeat the activity if is there is time and interest.

———

LESSON 3: ENCOURAGING POSITIVE COMMUNICATION (LISTED AS ACTIVITY #2 IN THE TEXT)

A series of three lessons, with the fully detailed format beginning on p. 99 in the main body of the text and concluding on p.111)

LESSON 3A: INTRODUCTION TO SUCCESSFUL LISTENING (P. 99 IN TEXT):

Objectives:

1. To describe and practice useful listening skills that help students to successfully engage in total comprehension during conversations.

2. To understand and avoid barriers to communication.

Anticipatory Set: As an introduction, you could offer the following questions to the class in considering the frequent problems many experience in communicating with others:

How well do members of our society listen to each other?

- How do you know when an individual is listening to you? (One can judge by behavior, body language, facial expressions, etc.)

- How do you know when an individual is *not* listening to you?

- How does one *feel* when a person is listening?

- How does one feel when a person is *not* listening?

- Why is it sometimes difficult to listen?

- What does it mean to *actively* listen? (Any responses similar to the behaviors listed under "Instruction" would be encouraging.)

- Why is listening important?

Instruction: Discuss the following basic listening requirements:

- Make solid eye contact and lean into the conversation, nodding when motivated to do so.

- Try to be accepting, even if you initially disagree.

- As the individual is speaking, use "cultural fillers" ("Is that right?" "I understand." "Really!" "Tell me more." "Uh-huh.") In this way, the speaker knows you are listening intently.

- Encourage more communication: "Tell me more." "Would you like to talk about it?" "How did you feel about that?" "Then, what happened?"

STOP LISTENING!

As a method of underscoring the importance of listening, ask a student to speak to you about an important topic. (Encourage him or her to choose a topic that is recent, significant, and known to everyone in the room). Role-play the "non-listener," the individual who makes minimal efforts, sounds and gestures, in letting the speaker observe that he or she is listening. When the speaker begins engaging the topic, behave in somewhat the following manner: Eyes moving quickly from side to side, head turning, glancing at your wristwatch or the wall clock, continually nodding much too quickly, shuffling papers on your desk, repeating, "Yep, yep," and making little if any real eye contact.

Following the verbal attempt, ask the speaker how he or she feels about your reaction. Responses have usually been something like: "Left out, not important, unsuccessful, like you didn't care about me or what I had to say,...."

Then ask the individual to engage in delivering the message again. This time hold still, leaning forward, maintaining eye contact, nodding from time to time, and using verbal "cultural fillers," (I see! / really! / hard to believe! / no kidding! / go on) as well as facial responses. Once again, ask how the speaker feels. I'm sure you can easily anticipate the dissimilar reaction. Listening is something upon which we all need to focus.

It is now time to introduce the effective **skills and barriers** below:

- **Reflective Listening:** Feed back to the speaker words that disclose how you perceive him/her. We must listen to the feelings behind the speaker's words. Sometimes, the *listener* ends up informing the *speaker* how the speaker feels. "Sounds like he made you pretty angry." "You seem really sad." "You sound anxious about this concern." "I'll bet that's very frustrating to you." "You really get angry when he says that, don't you."

- **Paraphrasing:** Let the speaker know that you've heard him or her by repeating the message in your own words. "So, you're feeling quite lonely right now because she told you she would call to plan the shopping trip and never called."

- **Summarize:** Highlight the main points. "Here's what I hear you saying..."

"If I understand you correctly, you're saying that...." _Condense it._

Barriers to communication may occur when the listener is responding to the *facts* rather than to the speaker's *feelings*.

- Do not offer quick solutions: "Quick-fix" remedies may give the speaker the impression that you think he or she is not "smart enough" to figure it out alone.

- Avoid making judgments: "You're taking this too seriously." "I'd just stop talking to her if I were you." This does *not* help.

- Do not minimize the problem: "I'm sure you'll feel differently about this in a week or so." Again, it is not the solution to the existing problem for the speaker.

- Don't *take the floor away* from the speaker by interjecting your experience concerning a similar problem: "The same thing happened to me; here's what I did."

The speaker is looking for someone, primarily, to listen to him or her; *listen* is the key word.

GUIDED PRACTICE:

Following the coverage of the above skills, instruct the class to develop a two-or three-minute message to verbally share with a classmate. The message could be based upon almost anything...opinions, events, sports, future plans in life,.... Then, explain the strategies listed on the next page (listener and speaker responsibilities), while demonstrating how to engage them. Students should, of course, be given sufficient time to study the task in preparing.

Divide the kids into groups of two, one being the speaker and one being the listener. Following three-to-five-minute engagements, instruct each of the two to feed back to the other thoughts and feelings concerning the exchange. What transpired? How did it succeed? Following that, reverse the roles. Another approach would be to have a duo go through the activity in the center of the room. Then, review the experience using comments from the entire class.

Listener

Focusing	Attending	Reaction
-Finds a purpose for listening.	-Decides whether message is organized.	-Asks for further clarification.
-Is prepared to deal with major distractions.	-Tries to anticipate speaker's point(s)— accepts or rejects them	-Feeds back major points.
-Is ready and willing to be attentive.	-Asks for clarification.	-Voices concerns constructively.
-Attempts to be open-minded.	-Evaluates -Remains sensitive to nonverbal messages.	

———

Speaker

Focusing	Attending	Reaction
-Prepares message with a purpose.	–Presents message in a clear and organized manner.	-Accepts and responds to questions.

-Decides what to say and how to say it.

-Speaks clearly with appropriate volume and speed.

-Is sensitive to listener's reaction.

-Feels free to use nonverbal communication.

-Is open to constructive criticism.

———

LESSON 3B: WHAT STOPS SOME STUDENTS FROM BECOMING ENTHUSIASTICALLY ENGAGED IN CLASS ACTIVITIES (P. 103 IN TEXT):

Objectives: To stimulate students' active involvement in daily lessons.

Anticipatory Set: Briefly discuss the connection between poor or mediocre involvement in daily lessons and inadequate achievement in school. How might this evolve into ultimate long-term effects?

Input: Begin a discussion centered upon the connection between success within the school environment and success in life. Briefly describe the potentially everlasting results of poor grades, the difficulty in furthering one's education, and acquiring a quality job. Underscore the difference in paychecks between possessing an unsatisfactory job and having well established, respectable employment. Stress the need to do whatever necessary in developing one's potential regardless of environmental circumstances.

CONSIDER OFFERING SOMETHING LIKE THE FOLLOWING:

"How important is college? Information from the Federal Government suggests a college degree is worth the time, work, and money invested. The vast majority of people with a college degree earn nearly twice the income of people with only a high school degree. Additionally, college graduates are more inclined to avoid layoffs and to be employed long-term. At the same time, we must clearly state that <u>every</u> student may <u>not</u> need to acquire a college degree. Valuable skills enable many to earn excellent wages while also allowing them to truly enjoy their occupations. These people must, however, sincerely work at learning their trades so as to be successful. And usually,..the learning <u>begins in school</u>.

Instruction:

Introduce and pursue the following topics:

A. What is it about *others* that stops me from becoming enthusiastically engaged in a class activity?

• Individual responses on paper. Grammar and spelling do *not* apply.

• Discussion with a partner. Share, discuss, make suggestions.

• Discussion in groups of four. Share, discuss, make suggestions.

• Class discussion.

• Instruct participants to silently write "Prescriptions." (This technique was introduced in chapter 6. Suggestions are made by classmates to help deal with particular concerns, then shared with the student experiencing the difficulty or with the entire class.)

• Teacher or student reads the responses. Further discussions at discretion of teacher and class. <u>Suggestion</u>: Walk the room during the earlier part of the lesson observing examples of the students' use of the Listening Skills.

RATIONALE TO LESSON:

It gives students an opportunity to:

- See evidence of others' frustration (I'm not the only one...).

- Relieve some of their frustration through discussions and venting.

- Discover solutions to their problems.

- See evidence of teacher's fairness, patience, understanding, and respect.

THEN...

B. What is it about *me* that stops me from becoming enthusiastically engaged in a class activity? Emphasize the importance of <u>honesty</u>.

Follow same process: Individual responses, discussion with partner, groups of four, class discussion, prescriptions.

<u>**Closure:**</u>

Discuss responses...

LESSON 3C: DEVELOPING THE CLASSROOM CONTRACT (P. 106 IN TEXT):

<u>**Objectives:**</u>

1. To empower students by having them take part in developing academic and social procedures as well as daily routines for the class.

2. To improve their motivational ambitions.

3. To create an atmosphere that will allow self-esteem and respect for peers to grow.

4. To enhance their educational experience.

5. To help them in accepting responsibility for making significant decisions.

6. To help them develop a greater appreciation for academic challenges.

Anticipatory Set:

Good teachers realize that students need to be empowered. Allowing students to have a measure of control over their daily classroom affairs strongly increases the chances of greater student participation, boosting their self-confidence and optimism, thus motivating them to take positive educational risks.

We can provide an atmosphere that will allow:

• Self-esteem to grow and prosper.

• Greater self-confidence.

• A more satisfying educational experience.

• Increased academic performance.

• Fewer absences.

• Increased morale.

Thus, allowing them to take part in developing classroom procedures benefits everyone.

What better way of boosting confidence and helping to create a positive classroom environment than through the use of a Contract whereby the kids, along with the teacher, participate in creating academic and social guidelines along with procedures for all to abide by in the coming year. Students retain far more from their active **involvement** in classroom activities than from traditionally teacher-led sessions.

Reflect upon Lesson 3b (What Stops Some Students From Becoming Enthusiastically Engaged in a Class Activity) by beginning with something like: "As we've pointed out, one thing that may prevent a student from enthusiastically participating in a class could be one or more of the other students; or it could be something that lives within the student himself/herself. Additionally, however, to be totally honest with you, it could be something that exists within the school environment or daily lessons, as well. I'd like to talk about this for a while."

Input: (Example)

"In the past, have you taken courses that seemed unappealing, absent of any enjoyment and true academic creativity;...or just not what you might have been hoping for.... ? Yeah, I know, more than likely. Have you taken courses that were just the opposite...courses that you looked forward to beginning, that brimmed with interest and excitement, lessons that you actually enjoyed? Yes, it does make a difference.

"Well, I'd like to do whatever I can to make this course one you'll remember in a positive way. In order to help us move in that direction, I'd like to develop a contract with you.

"As many of you may know, a contract represents two sides that come together to construct an agreement. What do you want to get out of my class this year? What are you hoping to gain? The answers to this question would be your side of the agreement."

Instruction:

With that, ask them to brainstorm aloud a list of "Gets" on newsprint, screen, or front board that reflect the type of class guidelines, routines, and achievements they wish to derive in taking your course. (These "Gets" may pertain to the curriculum or the general classroom environment and routine.)

Brainstorming: (Time-efficient technique) Students freely offer vocal suggestions with no raising of hands. Each proposal is recorded in full view of the entire class. This encourages total involvement in a discussion. Do not pause to evaluate a particular submission as to its plausibility; ideas may be analyzed at the conclusion of the activity.

Ask for clarification only when absolutely necessary, being careful not to put the student in a position where he/she feels that the contribution must be defended.

All suggestions are valid and written down.

Some common Gets suggested by students: Help with homework after school, individual help with the skill of mastering the subject matter, good grades, positive notes to parents, extra credit opportunities, homework passes, read novels that students select, spend time reading silently in class, go on field trips. Write all assignments in clear view and leave them there for several days.

Following the brainstorming, approach any suggestions that are unusable in a nonthreatening manner: Have Fridays off, play in the gym every morning, eat lunch in your room....

In approaching the un-usable suggestions, you could do the following:

- Point out that "Fridays off" would be frowned upon by the principal, superintendent, board of education, parents, etc. According to state law, it's also illegal. "Are there any other brainstormed items that would be impossible to attain and therefore, a waste of our time in pursuing?"

- You could suggest substituting something else. Rather than having Fridays off, perhaps use part of one class each semester to celebrate a holiday.

- Additionally, your own schedule would not allow you to eat in the room on a daily basis, but would you be willing to do it once or twice during the course of the year if it was possible to arrange? Making these types of concessions can display your willingness to work with the class and construct a meaningful Contract.

Next, disclose a prepared list of your additional contributions (your Gives):
- Time and energy

- Knowledge

- Respect

- Patience

- Humor...etc.

- One of my yearly contributions was: A trip to a community swimming pool taking place during an evening, with swimming from 6:00 until 8:00 for no charge. Parents would provide transportation with three to four kids per car, and we'd conclude by stopping at McDonald's following the swim. (Always incredible expressions.)

- Early Bird Special: (Quoted earlier) Created by my former colleague, Tom Murray. "On days when I plan to give a shotgun (a pop quiz), I place a bonus question on the board just beneath the map. At precisely thirty seconds before the bell rings, the map is pulled down to conceal the bonus question. Anyone arriving after this time will miss an opportunity to collect the bonus points." Along with this being a teacher give, "it will (also) encourage students to try to get to class as early as possible on a regular basis, especially since they do not know in advance when there will be a shotgun."

Disclose another list...the "Non-negotiables." – (Try not to make it too long.)
- No violence.

- No put-downs or bullying.

- No lying. Etc.

At this point, they brainstorm their list of, "Gives to Get." What are they willing to *Give* so as to receive their list of *Gets*? If, in your view, certain necessary class *Gives* are not suggested (homework on time, punctual arrival, attentive during class, etc.), ask that they put themselves in your position for a moment; what would they ask for if they were a teacher in charge of instruction? Or, if necessary, simply make a request.

Closure:

Finally, review all brainstormed items and discuss the Contract.

This activity establishes a climate of cooperation within the room. It also utilizes positive peer pressure in keeping fellow students on task and conscientiously committed to success. (And, of course, it's unconventional)

If the teacher faces a situation where a student is perhaps, uncooperative in some way, one may initiate a <u>private</u> contract with only that individual. This approach allows room for negotiation while leaving the student's dignity intact.

Treating uncooperative students with dignity not only generates greater potential for the development of their self-worth; it attains their attention in a positive manner while also modeling appropriate behavior that can frequently help sustain positive relationships within their group of peers and <u>with the teacher</u>.

LESSON #4. THE SEAT OF DISTINCTION (P. 113):

This activity can provide opportunities for students to engage in honest communication, reduce or eliminate self-disapproval, encourage peer acceptance and bonding, while discouraging injury to pride and egos through bullying or any other inappropriate behavior.

Objectives:

1. To open positive lines of communication.

2. To enhance self-esteem.

3. To give class members opportunities to hear sincere, complimentary messages.

4. To practice accepting compliments without attempting to deflect them.

5. To address the ramifications of pointless criticism and bullying.

6. To demonstrate our common needs.

7. To reduce or eliminate self-disapproval.

8. To break barriers and enhance relationships.

9. To underscore the reality that every classmate possesses positive qualities.

<u>Anticipatory Set:</u>

Role-play an example of strong criticism with a student who's been made aware of the lesson's objective and has consented to taking part in the role-play (discussed with student earlier; the remainder of the students should be unaware that it is simply an act)

Example:

"Bruce, you've forgotten your homework again! You're nothing more than a failure! Why can't you be more like Mary?" (Voice somewhat raised)

After a brief moment, make the class aware that it is a role-play.

Perhaps reveal its purpose by dropping a rolled sheet of newsprint or exposing a question written on a Smartboard....

"What may the result be if a person frequently hears severe criticism?"

(Perhaps, address Bruce in a manner similar to the following: "We really had them believing it, huh, Bruce. You were great. Thank you.")

Have class brainstorm responses to the question.

Examples:

"He'll feel dumb." "She'll really begin to believe it." "He'll have little self-confidence." "She'll withdraw, not do well in school, not want to participate, want to do harm to himself," etc.

Input:

Discuss the following questions thoroughly, giving appropriate examples:

1. What's it easier to do, criticize or compliment someone? (Obviously, criticize.)

2. Why is it that when we are genuinely impressed by one's behavior, we seldom communicate that impression to him or her?

3. How do you feel when someone says something nice about you?

4. Why is it that when we receive compliments, we sometimes deflect the praise?

Instruction: The Seat of Distinction: Explain that each class member will have the opportunity to receive positive messages from classmates when sitting in "The Chair."

GROUND RULES

1. All compliments must be of a sincere and honest nature; they must deal with personal achievements or qualities, not with appearance ("I like your sneakers").

2. Chair occupant may not respond to messages in any way other than saying, "Thank you." (If not inclined not to say, "Thank you," they should remain silent). This prevents students from deflecting a compliment; they *must* accept it.

3. Appoint five students to collectively sit apart from the class (on the side of the room, perhaps). These people make up the "Praising Panel." Their responsibility is to express *sincere, positive* messages to the chair's occupants. The teacher should encourage members of the Praising Panel to call the occupant by name and maintain eye

contact. This personalizes the praise and allows it to be sincerely "felt" more keenly by the student sitting in The Chair.

Caution members of the Praising Panel to begin thinking of an honest compliment as soon as they know who will be occupying The Seat of Distinction. In this way, youngsters do not suddenly find themselves unprepared to share a sincere word of kindness. "I can't think of anything" is certainly counterproductive.

4. Eye contact – extremely important. Demonstrate by complimenting a student while not facing him or her and then again while maintaining eye contact. Ask which time the compliment felt more meaningful.

5. Other members of the class may then follow the panel with additional positive messages directed to the chair's occupant.

6. At conclusion, ask the occupant of The Chair:

   a. "How was the experience?" If the student responds, "Embarrassing!" ask, "Embarrassing-Good or embarrassing-Bad? Weird-Good, or Weird-Bad?" etc.. (Ask students to clarify when necessary.)

   b. Ask the occupant, "Did you hear anything that you didn't expect to hear? (Share it or pass) Though peers may not frequently exchange positive comments with each other, they more than likely, *do* have complimentary thoughts of their classmates, and it's worthwhile taking the opportunity to vocally offer them. Drive this home.

   c. Finally, ask the departing seat occupant, "Who'll be the next classmate to occupy the 'Seat of Distinction?'"

After the student in the chair selects the next occupant, he or she taps a member of the Praising Panel out and replaces that individual as a "complimentor."

Closure: When all have occupied the chair, promote a discussion based upon the lesson's objectives 1—9.

- Following the experience, continue to listen for daily exchanges that reflect the main points of the lesson.

  a. Students' intentions should be to offer comments that-

     - demonstrate respect for themselves and others.

     - demonstrate personal and social responsible behaviors.

     - acknowledge the benefits of accepting praise from peers.

     - express the idea that deflecting compliments serves no one's best interest.

     - acknowledge our common needs for social acceptance.

     - recognize that treatment affects one's feelings, self-confidence, and academic and social success.

     - identify the need for tolerance, understanding, and empathy.

     - reflect the idea that when complimentary thoughts occur, they should most often be expressed.

     - accept the idea that compliments "feel good" to the complimentor as well as the person being praised.

     - acknowledge that it's very easy to criticize.

a. Consider assigning an essay on The Seat of Distinction.

b. Students may pair up in groups of two and discuss the experience by applying active listening skills.

c. Observe the social interaction of your pupils to determine the impression made by the activity.

d. Students may discuss behavior changes observed daily that they believe can be attributed to experiencing the lesson.

STUDENT

(unspoken words)

My grades could be higher; I admit it.
But that doesn't mean I don't appreciate your concern.
When you're near me, I may feel a little nervous,…
But that doesn't mean I don't want you to come closer.

I know I don't smile when you approach,
But please don't stop smiling at <u>me</u>.
I may not respond to your greetings, but your
Words of encouragement have become part of my life.

When you pause at my desk, your hand rests on my shoulder.
Though I don't know how to return
Your offer of warmth and friendship,
Please don't allow that to diminish your comforting support.

You're older…and your clothes are neater than mine,
But,…you make me feel,…I don't know…
Like…like you're my <u>friend</u>.

I'm always happy to be here….in your classroom.
In fact, at the end of the day, I don't want to leave (don't tell Mom).
When the year ends, and I don't see you every day,…
I know I'm not going to like that…I don't want it to end.

V. Sgambato

ENDNOTES....

1 "Second Order Change," Super Teams Limited p. 16
2 "Tell Me and I Forget," Northeast Regional Center for Safe and Drug-free Schools for the US Dept. of Education. P. 48
3 "Prescriptions," Super Teams Limited p. 91
4 "Listening Skills," ibid, p. 102
5 "The Milling Assassin," Patricia J. Kimmerling, <u>Teaching Strategies for Values Clarification</u> (May 1, 1974) p. 107
6 "Processing the Activity," Super Teams Limited p. 109
7 "Encouraging Positive Communication," ibid, p. 118
8 "Affective Classroom Contract," ibid, p. 126

AUTHOR BIOGRAPHY

Vic Sgambato has thirty-five years' experience teaching English, writing, and health. In addition to publishing articles on education, history, and health and wellness, he's assisted in developing a curriculum resource guide to support the new learning standards in health education for the New York State Department of Education. Sgambato also developed curricula for the Fort Plain Central School district in the areas of English, health, and AIDS education.

Additionally, he was:
- Fort Plain's June 1997 Teacher of the Year.

- A recipient of the 1998 New York State English Council **Educators of Excellence** Award.

- A 1992 New York State Teacher of the Year nominee.

- Nominated and accepted three times for inclusion in *Who's Who Among America's Teachers*.

- Former trainer for the A World of Difference Campaign directed by Neal & Jane Golub.

Now retired from education, Sgambato lives with his wife in Fort Plain, NY. They have four grown children, seven grandchildren, and one spoiled chocolate lab.

25448811R00118

Made in the USA
Middletown, DE
30 October 2015